No Bacon and Eggs Tonight

By

John Heath Brook

First published 2002 by Creativelines, 54 Cedar St Southport Lancashire PR8 6NG
in conjunction with the author.

Copyright © 2002 John Heath Brook

ISBN 0-9542841-0-0

All rights reserved. No part of this publication may be reproduced, stored in a retrieval system, or transmitted, in any form, or by any means, electronic, chemical, mechanical, photocopying, recording or otherwise, without the permission of the publisher.

Contents

Dedication
Introduction and Acknowledgements
About the Author

Chapter	*Page*
1) *"Abracadabra! Jump! Jump!"*	*1*
2) *The Beginning*	*3*
3) *Selection Board*	*7*
4) *Call Up*	*9*
5) *Square Bashing*	*12*
6) *Training Begins*	*15*
7) *South Africa Bound*	*21*
8) *No. 44 Air School Grahamstown*	*24*
9) *Homeward Bound*	*30*
10) *Teddy Edwards and Crew*	*33*
11) *50 Squadron ~ Skellingthorpe*	*40*
12) *617 Squadron*	*53*
13) *June 24th ~ Day of Destiny*	*63*
14) *Prisoner*	*65*
15) *Oberursel Interrogation Centre*	*81*
16) *Stalag Luft 7 ~ Bankau*	*97*
17) *The Forced March*	*130*
18) *Stalag 111a ~ Luckenwalde*	*145*
19) *Freedom (or is it?)*	*159*
20) *Rendezvous*	*170*
21) *Journeys End*	*173*

Epilogue

" I dedicate this book to the memory of my crew mates and comrades who were killed in action on June 24th 1944, and who now lie buried but never forgotten in France:

Pilot & Skipper	John Andrew Edward ("Teddy Edwards")
Flight Engineer	Bill King
Rear Gunner	Sammy Isherwood
Mid Upper Gunner	James Ian Johnston
Front Gunner	Tom Price

Teddy, Sammy and Tom are buried in the village churchyard at Leulinghem. An inscription on the graves reads 'I will lift up mine eyes unto the hills from whence cometh my help'.

Ian and Bill are buried at the War Graves Cemetery, Longuenesse, near to St Omer."

Introduction and acknowledgements:

"I first thought about writing about my wartime experiences when I retired from work, and having completed all the outstanding DIY jobs around the house, I found myself with time on my hands. So, borrowing my daughter's typewriter, I set up office in the back bedroom.

My thanks go to my wife José for putting up with the inconveniences and long absences, whilst I pounded away on the typewriter behind closed doors. Her understanding and encouragement meant so much to me.

My thanks also to my late sister Dorothy, who gave me such great assistance in setting out the contents in chronological order. I know that if she were still with us, she would be thrilled to bits on seeing it completed.

To Gerry Hobbs, my former wireless operator and surviving crew mate, my thanks for all the photographs and correspondence over the years, especially those relating to the burial of our comrades and the huge part played by Andre Schamp, the French farmer who was first on the scene at the crash site.

Thanks also to Bill Turner for the wonderful cartoons and portraits which he drew for me whilst we were in the PoW camps, some of which I have used to illustrate this book.

To everyone else who has helped in some form or another, my sincere thanks.

Above all, a special word of praise and thanks to my daughter Carol, and son-in-law Trev. Without their hard work and expertise with the editing and origination, none of this would have happened and my manuscript would have continued to gather dust. My sincere gratitude to you both."

About the author

John Heath Brook, was born in Southport on the 28th April 1921, the only son to Ernest Edward, an optician, and Eleanor Maud Brook. He had three sisters, Dorothy, Eileen and Anne. To his family he was John, but to most people he was known as 'Jack' or 'Jackie'.

After being educated at Linaker Street Primary School and King George V Grammar School, Southport, he commenced work in 1937 as a trainee technician at the Wolverhampton branch of the Post Office Engineering Department.

He volunteered to join the RAF in 1941, and flew on 37 operations as a bomb aimer, until his crew were shot down over France in 1944. He remained a Prisoner of War until 1945.

After the war he returned to work at the Post Office Telephone Engineering Department, later to be known as British Telecom, in Southport. He retired from his post as Senior Technician with BT in 1983, receiving the Imperial Service Medal. This was awarded for 45 years continuous service to his country, incorporating his service in both the RAF, and what was then a civil service occupation.

In May 1949 he married Josephine May Green, aged 24, at St Philips Church, Southport, and their daughter Carol was born in April 1963.

1

"ABRACADABRA! JUMP! JUMP!"

My heart was pounding as I clipped on my parachute, and beads of sweat formed on my brow. I had rehearsed this moment in my mind's eye many times over during my operational career with Bomber Command, at the same time secretly praying that it would never happen. My shaking hands fumbled for the safety handle of the escape hatch in the floor of the now stricken Lancaster.

I lifted the cover and tried to jettison it through the exposed hole, but no matter how I tried to push it out with my hands, the force of the air outside proved too strong, and the hatch cover stubbornly refused to drop free. I was becoming more and more panic stricken as precious time went by. Was this how it was going to end, all of us trapped, and about to be burnt to death in this blazing shell which used to be a proud bomber aircraft? Time was running out, and if I did not jettison the hatch soon, we were all going to die.

In desperation, I turned the cover on its end, and gripping the metal spar of the front turret to give me greater purchase, I stood on the cover and pushed with all my strength. Suddenly it was gone, and I was faced with a gaping hole in the floor of the aircraft. All at once, I was also faced with the new and very real fear of launching myself out into space and the unknown. I knelt on the edge of the hole, as we had been told to, willing myself to roll out and desperately trying to control my jagged nerves. I realised that the longer I waited the less chance anybody had of getting out alive. I tried to remember the drill - jump out headfirst, and count to ten before pulling the rip cord of the parachute.

By now the Lancaster was in its death throes, shuddering from nose to tail, and it would soon be plunging earthwards and out of control, with Teddy Edwards, our skipper and pilot, powerless to do anything about it.

It was now or never and closing my eyes, I rolled out head first into space. The noise of the onrushing air was deafening. I started to count; one.....two.....three..... Would the chute open? Or would I carry on in my headlong flight to the earth below? I don't think I reached the count of ten before pulling the release cord on the chute. There was a tremendous jerk as the canopy opened, and my dive was checked. I found myself swinging from side to side like the pendulum of a clock until I came to rest in a vertical position once more, with the sky above me and the earth below.

As I floated gently downwards, my thoughts went back to the Battle of Britain, and the start of it all, when I decided that I wanted to be a fighter pilot and fly Spitfires.

2

THE BEGINNING

I was twenty years old and the Battle of Britain had been fought out over the skies of south east England during that wonderful hot summer of 1940. Like so many young men of my age, I wanted to fly, inspired by the exploits of those pilots flying their Hurricanes and Spitfires in that epic battle during the months of August and September. Although numerically outnumbered in both men and planes, the pilots of the Royal Air Force inflicted such losses on the German fighters and bombers that they were forced to abandon all ideas of invasion.

I imagined myself as a fighter pilot engaging the enemy in dog fights over the Kent skies, and I was determined to volunteer for flying duties in the RAF just as soon as it was possible. It never occurred to me at this stage that I might not be accepted as suitable for flying. I suppose you could put that down to the arrogance and supreme confidence of youth. All that mattered was my desire to fly, and I was determined to achieve that goal come what may.

There did not seem to be any prospect of me joining the RAF in the immediate future. I was employed by the Post Office Telephone Engineering Department, now known as British Telecom, at their Wolverhampton branch. As such my work came under the heading of 'reserved occupation', which meant I would not be called up immediately for military service. However, I realised that if the war was to last any length of time, and it certainly had every appearance of doing so, then on account of my youth I would eventually be released for war service. This would probably be in the Army's Royal Corps of Signals, which seemed to be the branch of the services where most telephone engineers ended up. But I had made up my mind that flying was the job for me, and I would not settle willingly for anything else. I made extensive enquiries, and found that if I volunteered for Air Crew duties with the RAF then the Post Office would have to release me.

Fortunately for me, I knew a few lads who had undergone the selection board, not all successfully I might add, and I pumped them for information about what might lie ahead. I would have to sit a written examination in both maths and English, followed by a medical examination. Then there would be an interview to assess my true motives for wanting to join Air Crew. I had heard of cases where men had failed the interview because when asked the question "Why do you want to fly?", they had replied that they were attracted to the extra flying pay. I suspected that this was not the type of answer the interviewing officer would want to hear!

I did not anticipate too much trouble with the exams as although it was four years since I had left school, I had continued my studies by attending night school as part of my training with the Post Office Engineers, and had gained certificates in maths and telephony, which included physics and technical drawing. However, I was less confident about the medical examination which I understood to be very thorough indeed.

I was a keen footballer, and played for the Post Office team, so I suppose I was reasonably fit by ordinary standards, but I was not satisfied. I wanted to improve more in 'wind and limb' to give myself every chance to get through the medical. I realised football would not be enough, and I would have to devise other means to improve my fitness.

Although my official headquarters were at Wolverhampton, my place of work was for the time being at Dudley, a medium sized town approximately seven miles away. I decided that if I were to cycle to work, not only would I save the bus fare, but more

The Beginning

importantly it would give me the extra exercise that I needed. I had always been a keen cyclist dating back to my school days, and I had a good sports cycle lying at home, which my mother had bought me when I attended the local grammar school. I think she had a bit of a shock when I asked her to send it by rail to Wolverhampton! When it eventually arrived, it was badly in need of cleaning and servicing, as it had not been used for three years. It kept me busy for a week, working in the evenings, but at the end of all my hard work, it was as good as new, and after fitting a dynamo lamp, I was ready for the road. I came in for some leg pulling when I announced to my fellow boarders that from the next Monday I was going to cycle to work!

I must admit there were occasions when I felt like packing it all in, especially when it was pouring with rain, but whether it was pride, or just pure stubbornness on my part, I persevered and gradually my tired and stiff joints began to ease by degrees, and it seemed that the hard work I was putting in was beginning to pay dividends. At any rate my fellow boarders no longer made any wise cracks. After several months I no longer puffed like an old traction engine, and my muscles were free from pain. For the first time in my life, I positively glowed with fitness.

I had learned that one of the medical tests to be encountered was designed to test the lung power of the applicant. It consisted of blowing down a rubber tube, which in turn was connected to a graduated tube containing mercury. The object of the exercise was to blow down the tube, and raise the column of mercury to a given position on the scale and hold it there as long as possible. I had been warned that it was no easy matter, and that you felt as if your lungs were about to burst. It was impossible for me to get hold of a mercury tube to practice with, but I hit on the idea to attempt to inflate a football bladder. I was not very successful, and would go red in the face with my exertions, which used to frighten the landlady, but nevertheless it was all good practice.

Another medical test was designed to examine your sense of balance and co-ordination. The applicant had to close his eyes, and then stand on first one leg and then the other for as long as possible without losing his sense of balance. It sounds easy, but it took some concentration to remain steady for any length of time.

I am the first to admit that any stranger who happened to witness my daily exercises of standing on one leg whilst blowing up a football bladder, would have been entitled to think that I was a bit strange in the head. But I refused to be deterred, and from now on, the most important thing was to ensure that I maintained my present standard of fitness until I received notification to attend the selection board.

3

SELECTION BOARD

There must have been fifty men reporting on the same day as myself, all of us determined to give it our best shot. The maths questions were easier than I expected, requiring no lengthy workings out, and I finished in good time. The English paper included the writing of an essay, and my choice was "Why do you want to join the RAF?"

Having learned that I had so far been successful, the next hurdle was the medical, which contained all the tests I had been warned about. We were then told to sit on the floor with our backs to the wall and our legs stretched out. In front of us, and screwed to the floor, was a wooden beam representing the rudder bar in an aircraft. Obviously, you were intended to touch the bar with the ball of the foot. Most of the candidates could manage it easily, but yours truly, being on the short side, just managed to touch it with my toes. I shuffled myself down until the ball of my foot was just touching the bar, praying that the gap between the small of my back and the wall would not be noticed by the orderly who was walking down the line of men, making notes. For one moment I thought I might have got away with it until I heard "You seem to be having trouble in reaching the bar?" I replied that I could just about reach it, but he pointed out that I was not sitting upright, and to prove it put his hand in the gap behind the small of my back. He smiled at me and said "Good try, son!" and carried on down the line. From that moment, I knew I had blown it as far as being a pilot was concerned. After all my hard work, it looked as if I was going to fall down on the one thing over which I had no control - my height, or rather the lack of it.

All that remained now was the interview, and as I went in to see the Squadron Leader I tried not to show my disappointment. He told me that I had done very well in both the examinations and the medical. My spirits rose. Was I going to be selected for pilot training after all? However, he went on to ask if I would be willing to serve in a different capacity other than that of pilot. He understood my wanting to be a pilot - everybody wanted to be a pilot - but the RAF needed wireless operators, navigators and gunners as well. He believed that I was best qualified for training as an Air Observer, a role which combined the duties of navigator and bomb aimer.

As I travelled on the train back to Wolverhampton, oblivious to everything around me, I pondered on what had happened. I was upset that I had fallen down on what I considered to be a technicality. The interviewing officer had as good as admitted that with ingenuity I would probably have overcome any difficulty caused by my height. I had always considered a bomber pilot to be no more than a glorified bus driver flying from A to B. Flying as a crew member of a bomber seemed a much less attractive proposition to me than zooming across the skies in a fighter plane. But I gradually began to get things into perspective. Yes, I had failed the pilot's test due to something outside my control - that did not mean that I had not been good enough. By the time I reached Wolverhampton, I had come to terms with the situation, and all of my old enthusiasm had returned.

4

CALL UP

I was on my way at last, my civilian days for the time being behind me. I had said my goodbyes to my colleagues at work, and to my landlady and fellow boarders. I was entitled to a few days outstanding leave from the Post Office, and I had spent them at my home in Southport. My mother accompanied me to the station, where I boarded the train heading south for London. I could still see her waving frantically as the train finally cleared the station, and I wondered how many more mothers would be waving goodbye to their sons throughout the country that day.

Later, on leaving the tube station I saw several more young men of my age, all of us carrying cases and with gas masks slung over our shoulders, and all apparently heading in the same direction. The sight of these lads made me felt less isolated, and soon I was in conversation with a lad from Liverpool as we made our way to the reception centre at St Johns Wood.

We reported our arrival, were officially booked in, and then told to join the rest of the men who were standing in clusters outside on the makeshift parade ground. It is surprising how at the age of twenty, one can quickly form an acquaintance, and even the beginnings of a friendship, with people who were total strangers less than an hour before. In no time we had formed into small groups and were chatting together as though we had known each other all our lives.

No Bacon and Eggs Tonight

We were brought down to earth sharply by the sound of a loud voice bellowing across the parade ground, telling us in no uncertain manner to stop clucking like a lot of old hens, and to listen to what he had to say. He introduced himself as the sergeant in charge of our flight, and showed us to our barrack room with its rows of iron beds. He informed us that it was his job to lick us into shape and transform us into something resembling airmen during the next two months. He added, non too complimentarily, that from the looks of us he was going to have to work very hard to achieve that result, and that if he had to work hard, then we would have to do likewise. He made it quite clear that he expected a high standard of efficiency from us all, as he had the reputation of turning out the smartest and best drilled flight of the entire intake, and woe betide anybody who let him down. A few recruits dared to laugh, and he jumped on them like a ton of bricks. It was our first experience of a pep talk, and I am sure that in other barracks other sergeants would be delivering the same thing to their bunch of rookies.

We were then marched over to the stores to collect our uniforms and gear. Quite a lot of the uniforms needed altering, including mine, and were passed to the tailors. An NCO (Non Commissioned Officer) bellowed "What size hat?", and if you didn't know he would plonk different sizes on your cranium until finding one that stayed in place. It was a mad house, with NCOs shouting instructions to we poor bewildered souls; Shirts...2!", "Socks...2 pairs!" "Vests....2!", "Pants.......2!", and so it went on. There seemed no end to the amount of kit that we were being issued with. Boots and RAF greatcoat were included, and even the airman's best friend, the 'housewife', which was a slang term given to a small cloth bag containing a selection of needles, cotton and wool to be used in times of crisis - such as sewing on buttons and darning socks!

By now, as we staggered on down the line, we resembled pack mules, with our pile of clothing getting higher by the minute. At the end of the line all these items had to be checked off against a list, and signed for. By now I was utterly confused, and it was a

Call up

great relief when we were handed a white sausage shaped kit bag and told to pack it all away, and return to the barracks.

Our sergeant then gave us a demonstration of the correct way to make our beds. The blankets and sheets had to be folded in a certain way when not in use, and then stacked on top of the 'biscuits', which were square shaped mattresses, three to each bed. But there was more to it than that. All the folded blankets had to be in line. Standing at one end of the room the sergeant sighted the line of beds on one side of the room, and if one was out of line, it would have to be adjusted until it conformed. There was a well used service expression that covered this type of exercise admirably - a "load of bull". "Bull" was an occupational hazard which seemed to follow service men throughout their careers. However, it was a way of instilling a bit of well needed self-discipline into us.

As I lay in bed that night I realised that my whole life style was about to change. I had lost my civilian identity, and had become John Heath Brook No. 1575148. There was no going back now, even if I had wanted to. I was now a member of his Majesty's forces, holding the lowest rank in the RAF, in airman's terms an 'erk'. I wondered what tomorrow had in store, and drifted off to sleep.

5

SQUARE BASHING

We were woken at 6 am, and soon found ourselves outside in the cold morning air, half naked, in PT kit. We may have felt chilly at first, but the sergeant soon led us into a series of exercises, including running on the spot, with our arms threshing around like windmills. After twenty minutes of this we were dismissed for a shower and shave with our bodies glowing like coals. After breakfast the barracks were inspected for cleanliness. The sergeant was not too impressed with our attempts at bed making, and so we received yet another session of training, before going over to collect our uniforms which had now been altered.

All barracks had a leader to act as the liaison between the sergeant and the rest of the men. The sergeant immediately appointed an RAF corporal to carry out this role who had previously been a regular wireless mechanic on the ground staff. Having now been accepted for air crew training as a wireless operator, he found himself on the 'square bashing' course designed for new recruits. Despite his rank of corporal, he never pulled rank with any of us, and he always did his fair share of the chores. He was in his late twenties and we often turned to him for advice, and his experience was invaluable. When preparing for daily inspection, he told us where to dust, such as under the window sills, tops of door frames - all the places we rookies would not have thought to check. He helped us with our bedding and showed us how to polish our boots until you could see your face in the toe caps. As a result of his help our barracks were just about the most efficient of the whole intake.

Whilst the rest of us spent our evening in the NAAFI, or playing cards, the corporal would don his best set of blues and disappear for the evening. Although he was married, we suspected that there was a girl involved. We all envied the knife edge creases in his trousers and wondered if he had an electric iron hidden in his kit. We were amazed one night to see him take off his trousers and turn them inside out. He took a bar of soap, wet it under the tap, and then rubbed the wet soap up and down the creases of his trousers. He then turned them right side out again, and then very neatly folded them in their creases. He then proceeded to lay the trousers under the 'biscuits' on his bed before turning in for the night. Needless to say it wasn't long before we were all sporting knife edge creases in our trousers.

However, there was one area where our corporal friend could not help us too much, and this was in the endless hours of square bashing in the drill square. I well recall the disasters that befell us on our early sessions. I can hear the sergeant's bellows even now. "What's the matter with you lad? Have you got two left feet?" There were many more choice remarks, most of which are unfit to print. At first we thought it amusing when we kept bumping into each other, but after being given extra drills and constantly being on the rough edge of the sergeant's tongue, it began to look less funny. The offending culprits were told by the rest of us to 'pull their fingers out', and the standard began to improve.

If any of us had been homesick at first, by now we were too busy to let it worry us. We were constantly on the move. What with PT, square bashing, arms drill, barrack room inspections, we never had time to be bored. We must have been putting some energy into our work because by now buttons were working loose and holes appearing in socks. Although some of the men became quite proficient at such emergency repairs, I am afraid I was a duffer, and made hard work of it, quite often almost sewing the button onto my finger.

As the weeks rolled by our performance on the parade ground improved out of all recognition, and we could all accomplish the intricate drills, including presenting arms correctly without dropping the rifle! Perhaps more importantly we had learned to obey orders without argument, and were far more disciplined.

The night before we were to be posted to Initial Training Wing (ITW) at Torquay for the next stage of our training, the sergeant came to the barracks to individually wish us well. A nice gesture from a hard bitten regular drill sergeant, who clearly obtained great job satisfaction from transforming each squad from novices into well disciplined airmen. Tomorrow, he would be receiving his next intake of rookies, and I didn't envy him in the slightest.

6

TRAINING BEGINS

Torquay had virtually been taken over by the forces and was to all intents and purposes a garrison town. We were billeted into what would have been one of the premier hotels on the sea front, but which was now somewhat austere, having been stripped of all its trimmings. The heavy curtains had been replaced with blackout shutters, but there was still a fine view of the beach from the front windows. The only problem was that the beaches were now mined, fortified with barbed wire and anti invasion barge traps and were out of bounds.

I had assumed that at this stage in our training there would be some relaxation as far as PT and drills were concerned. It was not to be. Parts of the promenade had been taken over for drill practice, and the hotel forecourt was where we would undergo our morning PT sessions. Now that we had started our air crew training we had been issued with broad white belts and white flashes in our forage caps, which now meant extra work in the evenings keeping them white with a tin of Blanco. Woe betide anyone who went on parade with their belt and flash anything less than dazzling white.

Our classes were held in various other buildings and hotels along the promenade, and we were marched from one class to another at double time with arms swinging like pistons in unison. At this stage both pilots and navigators alike received the same instruction in maths, elementary navigation and meteorology, Morse and aircraft recognition. For me, Morse was the hardest part of the whole course. We all had to learn the code so that we could

No Bacon and Eggs Tonight

transpose any letter automatically, and had to practice sending and receiving messages in pairs using a buzzer and lamp. The trainee wireless operators suffered the most because they were expected to achieve higher speeds than the rest of us. I was relieved to receive a final assessment of average in everything, including Morse.

Having completed this stage, it was now the parting of the ways for most of the group. I along with the rest of the navigators would be posted to EAOS (Elementary Air Observers School) in Eastbourne, whereas the others would be going to their respective schools. From now on we would all delve deeper in to the complexities of our individual trades. It was with regret that I said my goodbyes, particularly to our helpful corporal friend. We had become very good friends on this course, despite our age gap, united no doubt by our struggle to learn Morse.

Jack Brook (far right) with colleagues at Torquay

Training Begins

Eastbourne was another garrison town, like Torquay. We stayed four to a room in the Grand Hotel, which was even more imposing than the one in Torquay, and the good news was that all the classes would be held in the hotel too. Here the training placed a much greater emphasis on the scholastic side. The time table would only allow one session of foot and arms drill down on the promenade per week. However, there were loud groans all round when we were advised that there would still be daily sessions of PT on the hotel forecourt before breakfast!

In the navigation class we were introduced to the mysteries of DR (dead reckoning navigation). This was a complex method of calculating wind speeds and directions, and how to use these wind speeds to work out the course for the pilot to steer. We had to plot the position of an imaginary aircraft on a chart using data given at different stages in the exercise, in the form of radio bearing or visual bearings, known as fixes, such as coast lines or rail intersections. When given data about changes in wind speed and direction which could blow the aircraft off track, we had to recalculate the course for the pilot.

We also started to learn the art of Astro Navigation, i.e. navigation by the stars, which involved taking shots of certain stars using a sextant, and transposing the resultant figures onto a chart to give your position. DR and Astro Navigation remained the basis of all navigation up to 1942 when the radar assisted aid, 'G', revolutionised navigation allowing for much greater accuracy.

Up until 'G', it has to be admitted that navigation was a somewhat hit and miss affair depending largely on the skill of the navigator, and weather conditions. Any navigator who has tried to maintain the bubble of the sextant on a particular star whilst the plane is bucking about will understand what I mean when I say that the most you could expect was an approximate position when using astro navigation. I think the nearest fix an average navigator could achieve would be between ten and fifteen miles. More planes failed to find their targets than did, and very often were forced to bomb secondary targets of their choice. In fact most raids only took place on moon lit nights, when visual fixes were more easy to obtain.

The boffins were well aware that details of 'G' would soon be in the hands of the Germans and a counter measure would be introduced. In fact eventually, the Germans were able to jam 'G' very efficiently using a type of interference we called 'grass'. But by this time it did not matter because other radar assisted aids such as H2S and OBOE were being introduced. Indeed, after modifications to 'G', it could once again be used accurately, even deep into the heart of Germany.

Such radar assisted navigational aids made it possible for hundreds of bombers to navigate successfully to any target in Europe, overwhelming the enemy's defences, and deliver their bomb load with reasonable accuracy in a very short space of time. This was known as 'saturation bombing'.

However, even with these navigational innovations, on night flights the target still needed to be adequately illuminated. And so in 1942, Air Chief Marshal Harris set up the Pathfinder Force. Their job was to illuminate the target by means of coloured target incendiaries. They were the first over the target and as such were exposed to the full force of the enemy defences, and as a result their casualties were amongst the highest in Bomber Command.

We were also trained in the theory of bomb aiming using a bomb sight, and taking into account wind speeds and direction. We learned about the different types of bomb; AP (armour piercing); HE (high explosive) and incendiary or fire bombs.

We also delved deeper into meteorology, such as cold and warm fronts, and cloud formations. We learned to avoid the giant cumulo-nimbus cloud shaped like a blacksmith's anvil at all costs as it could toss a plane around like a shuttle cock. On top of all this there was training in the instruments used on an aircraft such as compass, altimeter and air speed indicator.

Training Begins

Not surprisingly, time flew by and the end of the course examinations were soon in sight. It had been a difficult course and I was pleased with my final assessment of average in all subjects. As a result, those of us who had been successful, and not everyone had been, were now promoted to the dizzy heights of LAC (Leading Aircraftman). No longer the lowest rank in the Air Force, I looked forward to my well earned two weeks leave before moving on to the next stage in my training.

A Flight, No. 2 Squadron, No. 3 I.T.W., October, 1941.

7

SOUTH AFRICA BOUND

Trainee airmen could expect to receive their practical flying training in Canada or South Africa, as part of the Empire Training Scheme, or even in America. This tiny island of ours was no longer capable of handling the ever increasing number of trainees, and also there was the ever increasing threat of harassment from bombing raids from the German Air Force.

My first choice of posting was America, followed by Canada. I was not destined for either. We left Liverpool one damp cold morning on the passenger liner Arundel Castle bound for South Africa, my first trip on anything larger than the Mersey Ferry. I felt reassured to see so many naval ships buzzing like bees around our convoy of troop ships, protecting us from German U boats and aircraft. All the trimmings from this fine ship had been stripped to the bone leaving us with only the bare essentials, namely somewhere to eat and sleep. There was little to do except take part in the endless compulsory PT sessions and boat drills. Once the hooter went you had to drop everything and make for your allocated boat station complete with your "Mae West", or inflatable life jacket. We could walk around the decks, or attempt to play deck tennis, but the queues were so long that it was hardly worth the bother. There was fortunately a library, so we could at least read to relieve the boredom.

We were dreadfully overcrowded, with most men sleeping in hammocks slung over the mess tables at night. I was one of the luckier ones who managed to obtain biscuits, and I slept on the floor in any available space I could find. Life did have its lighter side, and the sight of the lads trying to master the art of getting in and out of a hammock caused great amusement. Unfortunately, in the early stages of this 'training', it was likely that someone would come crashing down on top of you at some stage during the night, whereupon there would be a mixture of curses and laughter depending on whether you were a victim or not.

After being on the receiving end once too often, I moved to join some of the other lads to sleep down in the hold. For several nights it was sheer bliss of uninterrupted sleep, but one night I was awakened by a scuffling sound. I shone my torch and to my horror a large rat was perched on the end of my bed staring at me, the light from my torch reflected in its eyes. This proved too much for me, and I let out an almighty yell. I don't know which of us was the more frightened, but it scuttled off to the depths of the hold. There were to be no more nights of sleeping down in the hold. Wild horses could not have dragged me down there. Even today I can still see those eyes reflected in the torch light.

As well as our sleeping problems, there were also many complaints about the food, which was never more than lukewarm by the time it got to us. But one thing that we had to be thankful for was that unlike most troop ships, the Arundel Castle was not a 'dry' ship. A large locker room had been converted into a form of off licence, and everyone was entitled to one bottle of beer per day. As quite a few of the lads did not drink, a thriving black market soon developed, with the teetotallers disposing of their allowance for a small profit.

As we approached the tropics, almost everybody lived in PT shorts and vest. Inevitably some of the lads failed to heed the warnings about excessive sun bathing, and as a result were forced to report sick with either severe burning or sun stroke. This is considered an offence in the forces, and the offenders were hauled up before the senior officer on a charge of 'causing self inflicted wounds'. They were dealt with leniently, only receiving a reprimand, but it served as a warning. By now the heat generated in the cramped messes was unbearable and I soon joined some of the other lads to sleep out on deck under the stars.

After about two weeks, we dropped anchor at Freetown to take on fresh supplies. Here a flotilla of small boats manned by young local native divers arrived alongside our ship. They spoke little English other than the word "tanners". What they wanted was for us to toss sixpences into the water, and they would dive gracefully, resurfacing with the coin between their teeth. Some of the lads tried to con them by wrapping pennies in silver paper, and the divers would resurface shaking their fists in disgust! Later, other locals arrived in boats with fruit for sale. We could get a whole basket of beautiful fruit for a few shillings and it made a welcome change from our lukewarm dinners.

This was our last stop before Cape Town, our final destination. There was great excitement on deck when the mists cleared and we caught our first sight of Table Mountain. I breathed a sigh of relief that we had been successfully shepherded here by the convoy Commander without any attack from a German U Boat. We had hoped to have some shore leave, but apparently convoys of troop ships were not exactly flavour of the month in Cape Town. Our predecessors had been allowed on shore, and the inhabitants had showered the troops with hospitality. Unfortunately, many of them had been on a 'dry' ship and went on the rampage, making a beeline for the bars, consuming vast amounts of alcohol, and picking fights with each other and the locals.

We had to wait until the following morning to disembark and we were loaded onto a fleet of trucks to take us to our transit camp. As we drove through the town centre, we saw for ourselves what damage our predecessors had done. The place was a shambles with whole sections of shop and hotel frontages boarded up. It was not surprising that we were no longer welcome, and it would be a long time before the people of Cape Town would forgive and forget. It was perhaps just as well that we were on our way to Johannesburg.

8

NO. 44 AIR SCHOOL GRAHAMSTOWN

I was destined for No. 44 Air School at Grahamstown which was about one hundred miles from Port Elizabeth in Cape Province. Although it was a fairly new school, at first sight it appeared impressive, with well built brick buildings. I had hardly unfinished packing before I heard an unmistakable Lancashire accent enquiring if there was anybody from Southport. His name was Les Ball and he was delighted to meet a fellow townsman. He was a member of the ground staff who worked on the maintenance of the planes. Apparently he had been asking that question for the last few months, and this was the first time he had had an answer in the affirmative. We went over to the NAAFI for a drink to reminisce about Home Sweet Home.

Our training began the following morning with instruction in the use of a parachute. The flight sergeant personally fitted and adjusted each man's harness, as it was important that it fitted correctly. Men had been known to fall out of their harnesses when baling out. We were led onboard an Avro Anson where a young South African pilot showed us how to use the intercom, oxygen supply and how to stow the parachute correctly. I had worried about whether I would be troubled with air sickness, but once in the air I was so busy trying to take everything in that I was being shown, that there was no time to feel ill.

The days now alternated between theoretical classroom work and our flying exercises. The Avro Ansons were dependable but very slow. But this made them ideal for trainees. We would work in pairs, one doing the navigation and calculations on the outward journey, whilst the other map read and obtained fixes, the roles being reversed for the return journey. At first I found it hard going and never seemed to have enough time to work things out, and frequently had to call for the assistance of our instructors. It was a great boost to our confidence when we managed to complete a full cross country run, returning safely back to base without having to ask for assistance once.

We also had chance to put our bomb aiming theory to the test over the bombing range. The bombs were smoke bombs, and from two large towers observers would take bearings on the smoke puffs to assess how close we had been to the target. This was my favourite part of the course, and there was plenty of friendly rivalry between us as to who could get their bombs the nearest.

There were also trips to the gunnery range which was out to sea at Port Alfred. Fairey battle bombers were used to tow a long sausage like object, a 'drogue'. Vickers machine guns were mounted in the turrets of our aircraft and we would have to fire at the drogue. I always felt sorry for the pilot of the towing aircraft, as judging by the standard of our shooting, he was taking his life in his hands. We were only expected to use the guns in an emergency, however, so thankfully did not need to reach the standards that would be expected from the air gunners.

The weeks rolled by and we continued to grow in confidence. After our mid term examinations, four of us who had explored Johannesburg together, decided to do the same in Port Elizabeth during our leave. We stayed at the YMCA, and it was through them that we met Mr and Mrs Roberts and their son and teenage daughter. They were a deeply religious family, hence their connections to the YMCA, but they never forced their beliefs onto us. We were invited to their home, and they were only too pleased to show us the sights. Through them we received many invitations, and made many new friends. Mrs Roberts quickly became a second mother to us during our stay.

No Bacon and Eggs Tonight

Batteries recharged, we returned to the camp for the second part of the course, which had an emphasis on night flying. Coastlines and water could be picked out in the moonlight, as could built up areas, but of course this was more difficult in wartime Europe where the blackout was strictly enforced. We had to rely more and more upon the wireless operator to obtain radio bearings, and astro navigation.

It did not seem long before we were facing our final night cross country flight, which was an important part of our final assessment. Still working in our pairs, the course was over four legs, base to Port Alfred, down to Port Elizabeth, then inland to Alicedale before back to base. We thought we had done well, until the instructor remarked that it was a pity we had been thirty seconds late! A more detailed assessment of our work revealed that we had never been more than two miles off track, had obtained two visual fixes, two radio fixes, one astro fix and had calculated four wind speeds and directions. Our log was up to date and all tracks and positions drawn on the chart. Despite the comment of the instructor, we were more than happy with our night's work. The written examinations would now be our final hurdle.

It turned out that we had all been successful, and I was pleased to get an above average assessment in both bombing theory and on the bombing range. Success in the examinations meant promotion to sergeant, and we received our Observer's Brevet the following week during the passing out parade.

It was traditional that the successful members of the course held a "Wings Dinner", in the presence of the Commanding Officer, and with one special guest each. Ours was arranged for Friday 9th October 1942, at the Grand Hotel. My guest was Les Ball, and we enjoyed an excellent seven course meal. Then came the serious business of the evening. We had been warned of the dangers of "Cape Brandy", a cheap and lethal local brew, but we felt we had plenty to celebrate, and that now would be a good time to sample it. I don't remember the journey back to camp, having passed out. I

No. 44 Air School Grahamstown

remember briefly coming to with Les standing over me with a cup of tea, and then went back into a stupor. It was the following evening when I finally came round feeling like nothing on earth. My only consolation was that all my fellow drinkers were in a similar state. To this day I have never touched brandy, and the very thought of it makes me ill.

    A few days leave were due to us, and so we visited our new friends in Port Elizabeth for the last time. Mrs Roberts was clearly upset as I suppose deep down she knew she would not see any of us again, and there were tears in her eyes as she told us that she would pray for our safety. She kindly re-sewed our brevets and sergeants stripes onto our tunics for us, making a much better job of it than we had. As it turned out, the observer's brevet was to take on a special significance. Ours was the last observers course at Grahamstown. There was a change of policy by the RAF and in future navigators and bomb aimers would become separate trades and thus would be trained separately. The Observer's brevet which took the form of half a wing with the letter 'O', would be replaced by half a wing with either 'N' or 'B'. All present holders of the Observer's brevet however would be allowed to wear it for all time.

Mr & Mrs Roberts and friends at home in Port Elizabeth entertaining John Brook and colleagues.

Wings ceremony and parade No7 Air Observers course 44 Air Training School Grahamstown South Africa

Top Left: Jack Brook & colleague Norman Batey in Cape Town

All other pictures are of Jack Brook at the Grahamstown Camp

9

HOMEWARD BOUND

It was with mixed feelings that we left behind No. 44 Air School for the last time. Our course was completed, but we would be leaving behind many new friends, both service and civilian, such as the Roberts family and their friends who had opened their homes to us, and of course, Les Ball.

We spent some time back at the Cape Town camp, until finally we heard that we would be sailing home in the Empress of Scotland. As this was a fast ship we would not be sailing in convoy. The troops on board were mainly newly trained air crew and some army personnel. There were also some American and Canadian seamen whose ships had been sunk. They, like me, felt more than a little apprehensive about sailing without the reassuring presence of the escort ships. Although we still had to sleep on biscuits on the floor, conditions were much better as there were relatively few of us on board. I did wonder if this was a deliberate ploy in case the ship was sunk, therefore minimising the loss of trained personnel. The ship was indeed fast and we had hoped to be home for Christmas, but due to mechanical problems we heard that the ship was to be diverted to dry docks in New York.

The cooks provided us with a traditional Christmas dinner, and then there was some good news for the British troops. We were to be temporarily billeted ashore whilst the repairs were carried out. We could not believe our luck. New Year in New York! We caught our first sight of the Manhattan skyline on the morning of the 27th December. After pay parade we were transported to our temporary home, an American air force base on the outskirts of New York. There was plenty of room for us as most of the men had finished their training and been posted away. Here we encountered a cafeteria, and wandering down a line with chefs serving food into different compartments on a tray appeared strange to us Brits.

Sight seeing trips were arranged for us by our American hosts, and I for one decided to take advantage of them. The views from the Empire State Building and the Statue of Liberty were breathtaking. An American sergeant also suggested that we might like to visit The Stage Door Canteen and along with one of my mates I decided to take him up on the offer one evening. The place was packed with troops, mostly American, and some were dancing to the music of Glenn Miller being played by a dance band on the stage. The canteen was sponsored by the stars of the stage, screen and radio, hence the name, and was run for the benefit of American and Allied forces and merchant seamen who were passing through New York. From time to time some of the big stars, such as Bing Crosby and Bob Hope, would give up their free time to entertain there. As soon as we arrived two young hostesses brought us some coffee and began chatting. The hostesses worked on a voluntary basis and were drawn from all branches of show business. Our two hostesses worked as secretaries in Radio City, New York. There was no shortage of volunteers apparently - in fact there was a waiting list. Perhaps many of them were looking to meet a future boy friend or husband. Certainly quite a number of romances had their origin at the Stage Door.

One of the girls invited us to a New Year's Eve party before leaving us to circulate around the canteen. That night I was careful to run the soap down the creases of my trousers. After all, it wouldn't do to go to a party with baggy trousers.

We managed to find our way to the address we had been given, and stood on the doorstep listening to the strains of the Glen Miller Orchestra from behind the door. Our hostess greeted us, and introduced us to the rest of the party, which consisted of her parents, other girls from Radio City, American servicemen and an English merchant seaman. The chairs had been pushed back to the walls to provide dancing space, and in the corner was a gramophone and a stack of 78s. There was a large buffet in an adjoining room, and cans of beer in the ice box. Needless to say we had a wonderful evening, but time caught up with us and we were soon toasting in the New Year and preparing to return back to the camp.

Two days later we were on the move again. This time we reached Glasgow without further incident. I eventually delivered Les Ball's parcels and letters to his family, even though it was a bit late for the festive season, but they were no less welcome because of that. For my part, it was good to see my family again, and I kept them all up into the early hours relating my experiences.

Unfortunately, as is always the case when on leave, time passed like wild fire and I soon found myself bound for the transit camp at Harrogate where I would stay until my posting to Operation Training Unit (OTU) came through.

10

"TEDDY EDWARDS AND CREW"

I had now reached the most critical part of my training, when the RAF would begin to find out if all the money that had been poured into my training would pay dividends. It was generally agreed that if a bomber crew could complete ten operations then the money spent was justified. In reality the life expectancy of the average crew worked out at less than ten trips, so Bomber Command was always in debt over the training of its crews.

The main topic of conversation amongst us was when and where we would be posted. Most of us were of the opinion that we were earmarked for Bomber Command, and that meant that inevitably we would join a four engined heavy bomber squadron. At this time we were all subject to self doubt as we faced the prospect of putting our training into practice. It was not just a case of being afraid to die, although that was always uppermost in your thoughts, but the fear of being found wanting at a time of emergency. I think we were all beginning to grow up and realise that there was nothing glamorous about going to war.

My posting came through and I was soon bound for OTU RAF Cottesmore, in County Rutland. At OTU we would sort ourselves into crews. Rather than being allocated to a crew, Bomber Command were currently adopting the policy of allowing the airmen to make up their own minds about with whom they wanted to fly. This system made for closer harmony amongst the men concerned, and it was easier to substitute anyone who turned out to be a misfit at this stage, rather than later. In such a close knit group of men, who were destined to live and fly together, there could be no room for any clashes of personality.

One day at lunch, a young air gunner with an unmistakable Lancashire accent asked me if I had crewed up with anybody yet. He told me he had been speaking to a wireless operator by the name of Gerry Hobbs, from Reading, who was looking to find crew members. He introduced himself as Sammy Isherwood and he came from Manchester. I was immediately impressed by his down to earth manner and felt at ease with him. He introduced me to Gerry and we soon found out that we had much in common, such as our passion for football. It transpired that Gerry had been talking to a pilot, John Edward, who was anxious to form a crew. However, he was an officer and was concerned that NCOs might prefer to team up with fellow NCOs. We told Gerry we were not concerned about John's rank, it was his skill as a pilot that mattered. With that Gerry arranged a meeting.

John Edward also came from the Manchester area, and at twenty eight was quite a bit older than us. We were all impressed by his quiet sincerity, and the upshot of the meeting was that we all agreed to team up with him as pilot and therefore the Skipper. The crew was later brought up to strength with Lorne Pritchard, a Canadian pilot officer from Moosejaw, Saskatchewan, Canada. John was usually known as Teddy Edwards, and so from now on, we were 'Teddy Edwards and crew'. We knew that if we were converted onto four engined bombers, we would need a flight engineer and an extra gunner, but for now our premier job was to try and get to know one another.

This was something that was actively encouraged. It was called crew co-operation and formed part of our training. Special comradeship and co-operation between individuals was essential if you were to get the best out of a crew. We called our officers by their first names when out socially, although mostly we referred to Teddy as Skipper. However, the fraternisation between officers and men was only to exist between individual crew members.

Irrespective of the mix of officers and ordinary ranks within a crew, the pilot was always Skipper and ultimately responsible for the decisions. Our Skipper was a strict disciplinarian when flying despite his mild manners when on the ground. He objected to unnecessary chatter over the intercom system. He also insisted that we should announce ourselves by our titles, such as 'navigator', or 'wireless operator', believing that the use of Christian names in an emergency might lead to confusion.

Although we worked hard, flying wasn't the only thing we were learning about. On a Saturday night we would make our way to Melton Mowbray, where we would partake of the local brew. As the weeks rolled by, our rate of consumption steadily grew. The local dance hall was always full of young Air Crew standing around the perimeter of the dance floor trying to pluck up the courage to go and ask one of the too few girls if she would like to dance. The local girls had never had it so good, being completely outnumbered by the men. They could afford to be choosy, and frequently were, but the state that some of us found ourselves in was enough to make any self respecting girl refuse (not always too politely) to dance with you.

Time moved on, and as we suspected, we were told that we would be joining a heavy bomber squadron, and so would have to master a completely new range of equipment. In fact we were to be posted to a Heavy Conversion Unit (HCU) at Swinderby, Lincolnshire, where we would be flying in Lancasters, the newest of the four engined 'heavies'.

The pilot was the man most affected in the conversion from twin engines to four. In the early war years, aircraft usually carried two pilots, one of whom was there to both assist the main pilot as well as gaining experience. As losses grew, Bomber Command realised this was a luxury they could ill afford, and dispensed with the second pilot. With the introduction of the four engined bombers, they introduced a new trade, 'flight engineer', whose role was to assist with takeoff and landing, as well as monitoring throttle and pitch settings, and calculating fuel consumption. He would be responsible for changing over to the reserve petrol tanks, as well as operating the landing flaps and retractable undercarriage.

The following morning after arriving at Swinderby our flight engineer was waiting for us. His name was Bobby McCullough and he was an Irish lad from Belfast. Before volunteering for Air Crew he had been on the ground staff as a fitter. We also met our new mid upper gunner who would take over the vacant mid upper gun turret. He was a French Canadian from the Quebec area of Canada, and, due to his auburn hair, was known as Red Cassaubon. Although they were the only members 'directed in' to the crew, we could not have chosen anybody better, and they immediately slotted in with the rest of us.

Our first job was to familiarise ourselves with the Lancaster, and I shall always remember our first encounter with the monster. I was overawed by its sheer size, and wondered how it could get off the ground and look as graceful as it did when in the air. The entrance was up a ladder, and through an access door just forward of the tail plane.

The rear gunner would then have to turn left, step over the tail plane spar, pass through folding bulkhead doors, then further turret doors, and then clamber in feet first, with the four Browning machine guns pointing directly aft. All the time he would have to try and avoid catching his parachute harness on any of the many projections along the way. With all the extra clothing that he had to wear to combat the intense cold, (including a specially heated jacket like an electric blanket) it was a work of art to get into the turret, and almost impossible to get out in an emergency.

Even if the rear gunner did manage to emerge from his tiny turret he still had to negotiate the Elsan chemical toilet, which tended to spend more time upside down than upright, and was situated by the bulkhead doors. Things were not much better for the mid upper gunner or front gunner, if it came to that. Few gunners escaped in a bale out situation, and the death toll amongst them was high.

Just forward of the turrets was the ammunition box with tracks leading the belts of ammunition to the turrets. In the floor was the flare chute used for launching flares to illuminate the target area, and for dropping bundles of 'window', which were strips of tin foil designed to jam the enemy radar devices. Continuing towards the nose you arrived at the main spurs which ran across the aircraft. They were high and wide and not easy to climb over especially when carrying equipment.

On the port side was an area reserved for the wounded, with oxygen bottles underneath. The wireless operator's position was in front of this rest bed, and in many ways was the best position on the plane. It was certainly the warmest, as it was adjacent to the warm air outlet. Immediately in front of the wireless operator was the navigator and his curtained off desk and 'G' set. Still further forward was the cockpit area, or flight deck. The flight engineer either sat or stood next to the pilot during the flight.

To get to the nose of the aircraft, and the front turret and bomb aimer's position it was necessary to squeeze yourself underneath the engineer's legs through a narrow opening. On a panel on the starboard side were sixteen bomb selector switches, and below, a timing device to be used if the bombs were to be dropped in a stick formation. The selector box determined the correct order in which the bombs were to be dropped from the thirty foot bomb bay. It was essential that the bombs dropped in such a way that the aircraft remained in a stable attitude.

Also on the panel were the camera and photo flash equipment which automatically photographed the bomb burst once the bombs had exploded. It was claimed that prior to the installation of this equipment some crews had jettisoned their 4000 lb. 'cookie' bomb over the North Sea in order to gain some height and avoid some of the flak and night fighters. The 'cookie' was a thin cased bomb shaped like an oil drum which would explode on impact creating maximum surface damage over a wide area. The flash circuit wiring was so arranged that a photograph would be taken immediately the bomb had been dropped. Any crew caught with a picture of the North Sea instead of the target area would be in real trouble, and unless they had a plausible explanation, would be facing a court martial.

Sometimes, crews would jettison their bomb load on an outward journey over the North Sea and then return to base. The reason for this was usually because a major mechanical problem had occurred. Aborting a trip in this way, or 'boomeranging' as we called it, always resulted in an enquiry. Some crews seemed to have more boomerangs than others and suspicions would be aroused. If it could be proven that a crew was in fact malingering, then a court martial would follow. If found guilty then they could be demoted, have their wings torn from their uniforms, and their pay books would be stamped with LMF. This meant 'lack of moral fibre', or in other words - yellow. I have no time for anyone who deliberately dodged their responsibilities, but clearly some men were simply suffering from operational fatigue. We referred to it as being 'flak happy', but it was no laughing matter.

Last but by no means least, was the master switch which had to be switched to LIVE in order that the bombs could be armed on their journey down to earth. I can sympathise with any bomb aimer who on checking the bomb bay on return from an operation realised that the bombs had been dropped 'safe'. The bomb sight was located in the Perspex nose of the plane, giving the bomb aimer a panoramic view of the sky and ground. To operate it, he would lie over the escape hatch found in the floor. He would line up the aircraft with the guide lines on the bomb sight by giving instructions to the pilot.

Above the bomb aimer, was the front turret with two Browning machine guns. Most night fighters liked to attack from the rear and below, so it was not normally manned. However, if under attack, the bomb aimer would have to switch to carrying out the duties of a gunner. After the D Day landings, when Bomber Command were called upon to take part in daylight raids, the front turret was manned permanently, increasing the crew to eight.

After the Skipper and Bobby had been declared capable of handling the Lancaster, we were ready for our maiden flight. We carried out the pre flight checks, and then one by one the mighty Merlin engines with their distinct and unique sound roared into life. The Skipper signalled to remove chocks, and we were ready to go. On receiving the green light from the control hut, the throttles were opened and we sped down the runway increasing speed all the time. "Full power!" roared the Skipper to Bobby, and between them they crashed the throttles through the gate until they were wide open. It seemed that the big black bird would never get into the air, and the perimeter fence was getting nearer. Suddenly the nose lifted clear and we were airborne. After a short cross country, the Skipper landed the plane with the skill that even a veteran pilot would have been proud of, and then taxied back to dispersal. We were all impressed by the Lancaster. I was struck by how stable she was, despite the immense power that she seemed to generate. The Skipper's face was wreathed in smiles, although he admitted that it had been the most nerve racking moment of his life. Far worse even than going solo in a Tiger Moth in his early days, mainly because of the responsibility for the rest of the crew. We were now ready to join a squadron, and soon we would be on our own.

11

50 SQUADRON SKELLINGTHORPE

We were to be joining 50 Squadron, at Skellingthorpe, about two and a half miles from the cathedral city of Lincoln. The cathedral itself was to become a familiar landmark. There was no more beautiful a sight than that of the cathedral at day break as it welcomed home the returning bomber from operations deep in the heart of Germany. My first glimpse of it in the early dawn always made me feel safe. However, it was important not to relax too soon, as the German Luftwaffe still mounted intruder raids on RAF airfields from time to time when the bombers and crews were returning home, tired, and not as alert as they should be.

Our sleeping quarters turned out to be very basic indeed, with twenty men to a large Nissen Hut. It was not surprising that we were to spend most of our free time in the sergeants' mess! From the windows of the lounge area in the mess there was a good view of the goings on of an operational squadron. On our first day we watched the armourers winching the bombs that were to be used on the night's operation into the bomb bays of the Lancasters. It was a sobering thought indeed to realise that we were in the middle of so much death and destruction. The petrol bowsers arrived to fill up the big black monsters with high grade aviation fuel. Although the target was never divulged until official briefing, the amount of fuel taken on board gave a clue as to whether the operation was of short or long duration.

The following morning a message confirmed that there would be operations again that night. Soon the ground crews were working like beavers with last minute repairs and alternations. This time our names were posted on the operations board and we left for the dispersal to carry out our night flying tests. I had the feeling that the ground crew were none too happy about a 'sprog' crew taking their beloved kite on operations, but it may have been my imagination.

In the briefing room, the curtains were opened to reveal the night's target. The Intelligence Officer gave his report on the defences we were likely to meet, and the Chief Met. Officer advised us as to the expected weather conditions. The Pathfinder Force (PFF) would drop route markers to assist with navigation, and we were reminded to bomb the centre of a cluster of markers to avoid the tendency for the bombs to fall short. The Signal Officer's details of the frequencies to be used and information from the Chief Engineer regarding petrol load, brought the main briefing to a conclusion. However, each trade then had to undergo their own particular briefing. The navigator's briefing involved working out pre-flight plans, working out the courses for each leg of the journey and plotting known enemy defences on the charts.

Soon it was time to don our flying suits and parachute harnesses, collect our parachutes, maps and instruments and leave for the dispersal points. We hardly spoke a word on the short journey. After pre flight checks we joined other aircraft from nearby squadrons in 5 Group Command and headed out over the North Sea.

As we neared the enemy coast we came under heavy fire from German Flak ships, but it was erratic and posed no great threat. Mercifully, the searchlights on the coastline did not pick us up. The first route marker had been dropped dead ahead of us which meant we were right on track, but from now on the gunners would have to be even more vigilant. As we travelled deeper into Germany we met with increasing flak but the route had been planned well and we missed most of the heavy concentrations. However, we saw some of the aircraft that had wandered off track going down in flames. Bomber Command's policy was to fly bombers in a compact bunch, the 'bomber stream', as a way of saturating German radar systems, hence any bomber that strayed from this narrow corridor would stick out like a sore thumb.

We were now on the final leg running up to the target, and the first coloured target markers were dropped by selected crews. We were scheduled to bomb on the second wave, and as we commenced our bombing run the flak increased in intensity, and anti aircraft shells exploded around us. The powerful searchlight beams lit up the interior of the plane, but we managed to complete our bombing run, adding our contribution to the scene of destruction which was rapidly unfolding before our eyes. The plane leapt into the air, as if with relief that the tremendous load had gone at last. Every now and then the unmistakable shape of a four engined bomber could be seen amidst the plumes of smoke below, clearly silhouetted against the back ground of fires which had broken out as the incendiary bombs took hold. The German defences, incidentally, had soon learned to take full advantage of this and frequently started decoy fires of their own, even to the point of using red and green flares amongst the fires. Luckily they could never quite match the colours!

The night's target was living up to its reputation as being well defended, and stricken bombers could be seen plunging earthwards. However, sometimes it could be difficult to tell if a plane really had gone down or not, due to another decoy which the Germans used. This was a shell which was fired into the bombing stream of the aircraft. It would explode with great ferocity, and give the appearance of a bomber being hit and set on fire, before breaking into pieces and plunging to the ground. I suppose it was a means to frighten us and put off any bomb aimer.

With the bombs dropped the Skipper was able to gain more height for the return journey. But although that put us above the flak, we were left open to attack from fighters who operated above this level. As we approached the coast, the skipper put the nose of the Lancaster down in a shallow dive, to build up his speed to enable us to cross the coast as fast as possible. But we had luck on our side and we made a safe return to base.

We could not relax yet though. We were debriefed by the Intelligence Officer about the concentration of flak, attacks by enemy fighters, and details relating to any planes that had been shot down. Eventually we were able to partake of the traditional bacon and eggs, which was always provided for returning air crew, before trying to get some sleep.

Although I was dog-tired, sleep seemed to evade me, as I tossed and turned, reliving every moment of the trip. I was not proud of being part of all that death and destruction, but I was not ashamed either, reminding myself that Germany had started mass bombing when they annihilated Warsaw, London, Rotterdam, Coventry and many other cities.

Air Chief Marshal Arthur Harris, Commander in Chief of Bomber Command, and otherwise known as Butch, was aiming to weaken the German resolve, but despite the efficiency of our bombing campaign, compared with that of Germany, bombing alone would not win the war. Contrary to Butch Harris's beliefs, the German morale remained firm until the end despite appalling loss of life. Critics of 'saturation bombing' forget that until early 1943, bombing was the only means of carrying the war into Germany itself. But all those who served in Bomber Command were politically snubbed after the war, and were not granted a campaign medal in recognition of their efforts.

As the operations mounted, we grew in confidence, and we survived the critical first five operations. Others were not so lucky. One of the crews who shared our billet failed to return one night. The RAF police came to collect the personal belongings of the missing crew, and although they were discreet and quiet it was not a pleasant experience for all concerned. I wish I could say it was an isolated case, but most crews experienced the trauma of losing their mates more than once. Sometimes crews were not around long enough for you to speak to them, let alone get to know them, getting the chop (going missing) after their first or second trip.

Air crew received very little practical training as to what to do when baling out. The accepted way was to leave the plane head first to avoid clouting your head on the tail plane. You were supposed to count to ten before pulling the rip cord on the parachute, by which time you should have been well clear of the fuselage. We were also told to bend the legs on impact, roll onto one side and release the parachute so as not to be dragged along the ground.

There was even less information available as to what sort of interrogation we might expect to receive if taken prisoner. We were told not to carry personal information which might help identify where we were flying from, and that the cells might be bugged. We were also informed of the Geneva Convention, which had been signed by Germany, even though it was often accused of only paying 'lip service' to its terms. This charter introduced a humanitarian code of practice. All uniformed men if captured should be regarded as prisoners of war (PoWs) and not spies, and were only allowed to give their number, rank and name when questioned. We were also warned about a bogus Red Cross form, which was actually a detailed questionnaire.

We did however regularly carry out dinghy drill, using a mock up aircraft, in case we were shot down over the North Sea. If crews were not to die of exposure, it was important that every man knew what part they had to play. The dingy would inflate automatically, but good swimmers would be needed to hold it steady, whilst the wireless operator would be responsible for the dinghy radio which was able to transmit the all important SOS signal. Other crew members were responsible for emergency rations, water, pistol and cartridges.

When we were not flying, or 'dicing' as we called it, life revolved around the sergeants mess as well as local bars in Lincoln. War time beer was not known for its strength, and due to rationing, many pubs often ran out. The sergeants' mess never seemed to run dry, however, and I suppose it was true to say that most crews indulged too much. Occasionally we would hold a Mess Party and Dance, usually during a prolonged spell of bad weather when all the aircraft were grounded. Station WAAFs and civilian girls were invited, and they usually degenerated into wild affairs. But even our parties paled into significance when compared with the goings on in the Officers Mess. Many a pint of beer finished up inside an officer's flat hat, and that was just for starters. It was certainly no place for prudes. But such excesses were a form of escapism for the horrors that we were never far away from.

Our Canadian gunner, Red, volunteered one night to take the place of a gunner from another crew who had gone down with a virus. The rest of us were enjoying a well earned stand down from operations and went over to the runway to see him off. His plane came thundering down the runway, but for some reason veered off, crashed and caught fire. By a miracle they all survived although badly burned, and Red was able to resume his career later on with a different crew. He was sadly to go missing on a subsequent operation, however. It came as no surprise that the replacement gunner for Red was the lad for whom Red had deputised on the night of the crash. His name was Ronnie Pooley from the London area.

We were now one of the most experienced crews on the squadron but this did not make us complacent. We attributed our success to a combination of luck and alertness. The Skipper certainly kept us all on our toes, which was to pay off on the night of the 23rd August, when we were scheduled for a raid over Berlin. Just as we started our bombing run, we were attacked at a range of some 800 yards by a Junkers 88 and Focke Wolfe 190. The accurate commentary from both gunners enabled the Skipper to take the correct evasive action, putting the plane into a series of corkscrew manoeuvres. The combined fire power from Sammy and Ronnie hit the JU88 and it fell away in flames, whilst the evasive action forced the FW190 to break off its attack.

No Bacon and Eggs Tonight

Later, on the night of the 27th September during a raid on Hanover we were once more attacked by a JU88. There was a repeat of the earlier incident, with Sammy and Ronnie again shooting down the JU88. Both these incidents were mentioned in the citation when the Skipper was awarded the DFC (Distinguished Flying Cross).

By now we were approaching the nervous twenties in our operational career, which was regarded as another critical milestone. After the magical thirty trip figure crews qualified for a well earned rest period well away from the operational scene. It was during this time, as well as periods just before ordinary leave, that crews often became over anxious or careless and as a result mistakes were often made that cost them their lives.

The one target that we feared the most was Berlin. Not only were the trips eight hours or more long, but the city was heavily defended. Running a close second was the Ruhr Valley, or Happy Valley as we called it, but only because the trip was shorter. The defences were just as strong if not stronger, as you had to run the gauntlet of guns and searchlights for at least twenty miles. The Germans had left a small gap in their defence system through which the bombers had to fly, and the efficient German night fighter pilots used to lay in wait for any unsuspecting bomber that might stumble into their path. If they were resorting to barrage or random fire, it was like playing Russian roulette and any crew was liable to be hit. The Ruhr was reported to have forty per cent of all the anti aircraft guns, and made heavy use of the deadly 88 mm anti aircraft gun, probably the best gun produced by either side during the war. No wonder we all trembled if our night's target was Berlin or Happy Valley.

The Germans had also built up a massive network of searchlights and sound locators from Northern Germany to the Low Countries, reaching fifty miles inland. German night fighters would also patrol this line, the Kammhuber Line, to attack any bombers illuminated by the searchlights. Unless the pilot took evasive action when picked out by a searchlight, you could find yourself caught in the intersection of three or more searchlights, and you would be a sitting duck. We called this being 'coned'. The only possibility of escape was to dive as steeply as possible which was not easy in a four engined bomber, and hope that the pilot could then pull out of the dive before the tremendous 'G' forces tore the wings away from the fuselage. I must admit I never met any pilot who was able to accomplish such a feat.

By late 1943 the German air defences were at their strongest and bomber losses were increasing. It was generally thought to be due to the success of the German fighter planes. Sometimes Bomber Command would send out diversionary raids, and the bulk of the fighters would be sent to the wrong target area, but the Germans were getting better all the time in predicting where the main point of attack would be.

This battle for supremacy would come to a head between August 1943 and March 1944. During this period sixteen raids were made on Berlin. Winter was the best time to attack Berlin, to allow the maximum hours of darkness, and quite often it was shrouded in cloud. As a result the PFF were forced to use the inaccurate sky marking technique, resulting in many bombs falling off target. The night fighters were growing in confidence all the time and by now the Luftwaffe had started to drop flares in the path of the bomber stream making it easier to pick us out visually.

The last of the sixteen major raids on Berlin ended with Bomber Command losing 72 bombers out of a total force of 800. This was put down to an underestimation of the wind speed. PFF calculated it to be 115 mph, but were sceptical of their findings and reduced it by 10 mph, and the Met. Office reduced it further. As a result the bomber force were way off target and wandered over heavily defended areas.

Just six days later, on 30th March 1944, Bomber Command suffered its heaviest losses yet in a raid on Nuremberg. Group commanders were horrified that the chosen route exposed the crews to a straight leg in the journey of 270 miles for over an hour. Harris insisted that the crews would have the benefit of cloud cover. Unfortunately, the weather changed suddenly, and the clouds rolled away. Even worse, white condensation trails which normally do not appear much below 25000 feet began to form. Also, it appears that some navigators never received corrected wind speed details. As a result many bombers dropped behind, and off track. So many bombers were being blown out of the skies that the navigators found it impossible to log them all. Ninety five crews were officially reported missing, a further twelve were so badly damaged that they crashed upon attempting to land, and a further fifty nine had to be written off. In one night we had lost 166 aircraft, and 750 men. By now, Air Chief Marshall Harris must have been the only man in the RAF who still believed he could win the war by bombing alone.

Our crew was destined not to take part in any of these ill fated operations or else we might have been part of those unwelcome statistics. However, we did find out that we were due to be posted to another squadron. We had the choice of joining either the Pathfinder Force or 617 Squadron.

617 Squadron had been formed especially to attack the Ruhr Dams under the leadership of Guy Gibson, and had continued its policy of attacking selected targets from low level at night. There had been two ill fated raids which had resulted in large losses, and the 'Dam Buster' squadron were in need of replacement crews. Of course, we knew more about the target marking role of the Pathfinder Force, than we did about 617 squadron.

We considered it a compliment that we had been asked to join either of these two special outfits, and after much soul searching we decided to throw in our lot with 617 Squadron. Perhaps we were becoming tired and disenchanted with the policy of bombing German cities. At least with 617 Squadron our bombing efforts would be directed on individual military targets, but to be honest I think we were also attracted to the 'glamour' that surrounded this now famous squadron.

So it was with real regret that we said goodbye to all our colleagues at Skellingthorpe and 50 Squadron. We had made many friends - and lost many as well. We were particularly sorry to say goodbye to our ground crew who had looked after and cherished our aircraft. At first they had regarded us with suspicion, but we had proved ourselves as a capable crew, and it was clear from their faces that they would miss us as much as we would miss them.

Sgt J.H.Brook

Dingy Drill ~ 50 Squadron

Rear L to R
FO. J. Edward   Sgt. Mc Cullough   F/Lt. L.Pritchard   Sgt. Cassaubon

Front L to R
Sgt. G Hobbs   Sgt JH Brook   Sgt S Isherwood

Crew members taken whilst at 50 Squadron:

John (Jackie) Brook on handle bars of bicycle, Ronnie Pooley astride bicycle, and Bobby McCullough about to launch secret weapon

Ronnie Pooley   Gerry Hobbs   Bobby McCullough

L/R:

*Sammy Isherwood
Ronnie Pooley
Bobby McCullough*

Taken whilst on 50 Squadron in Skellingthorpe.

L/R:

S.Isherwood

G.Hobbs

B. McCullough

Front:

JH Brook

12

617 SQUADRON

We were not the first crew to leave 50 for 617 Squadron. When Guy Gibson was forming his squadron, top of his shopping list were Henry Mawdsley and Mickey Martin, both from 50. Henry Mawdsley became one of his flight leaders but was killed on the Dam Raid. Mickey Martin was a small and chunky Australian who was regarded as just about the best low level pilot in the business. He could fly a Lancaster at tree top level without turning a hair. Whether his crew were as calm and collected as he was is another matter, but they must have had every confidence in him to continue flying with him. Flying at such low levels meant that he and his crew avoided enemy fighters and heavy flak concentrations, but apparently he would return to base with bits of telephone wires attached to his tail wheel. Mickey stayed in the Air Force until he finally retired, having achieved the rank of Air Marshall.

The Squadron was based at Woodhall Spa, and the living conditions were better quality than at Skellingthorpe. The billets were made of brick and partitioned off into small rooms. The Officers were quartered in the Petwood Hotel at Woodhall, which was comfort indeed. There was a long walk from the hotel to the aerodrome, but the officers thought that this was a small price to pay for the hotel's facilities.

Once again we felt ourselves to be very much the new boys amongst such illustrious company, even though we had completed over twenty operations. The Squadron leader was Wing Commander Cheshire. He was one of the most highly decorated pilots in the RAF and a Group Captain by the age of twenty five. So keen was he to resume operations that he gave up his command of RAF station Marston Moor, and reverted to Wing Commander in order to command 617 Squadron.

The squadron was in the process of changing its priorities from low level bombing to high level precision bombing on selected targets. We were to be issued with a new, and highly accurate, type of bomb sight. Squadron Leader Richardson was visiting the squadron to supervise the conversion to the new sight. He talked of nothing else, and soon earned the nickname "Talking Bomb". What he didn't know about the theory and practicalities of bombing was nobody's business. The object was to achieve an error of 100 yards or less from 18000 feet, which nobody thought was possible under operational conditions. His assistance was invaluable, and in time the best crews were achieving hits of under 60 yards from up to 18000 feet - and doing it almost every time - which made the rest of us try that bit harder to try and catch up.

The reason for this exceptional accuracy was soon revealed. A new huge bomb, designed by Barnes Wallis, who had designed the revolving 'Dam Buster' bomb, was to be made available. It was 12000 lb. with an aerodynamically designed tapered nose and offset tail fins, which caused the bomb to revolve. They were twenty one feet in length and had been named "The Tall Boy". They passed through the sound barrier as they fell, revolving at incredible speed. They would then corkscrew into the earth before exploding, the shock waves caused by this earthquake effect doing most of the damage. As they were so costly and heavy, only one could be carried, so it would have to hit the spot first time around.

Wing Commander Cheshire soon realised that precision bombing required a much improved system of marking. Cheshire and Martin had been toying with the idea of marking from a low level and had been practising diving their Lancasters over the sea to less than 1000 feet and then releasing marker bombs over a stationery target. They had found that they could achieve some accurate results. The mind boggles at the thought of diving a Lancaster to that height and then pulling out safely, but they were capable of it. The next stop was to convince Air Vice Marshal Cochrane who was 5 Group Commander that it could work under operational conditions. He discussed it with Winston Churchill who agreed somewhat reluctantly.

The chosen target was an aircraft factory at Limoges in France, where three hundred French girls were forced to work. Churchill insisted that adequate warning must be given to the French work force, and Cheshire undertook to take several dummy runs to give ample time for the workers to evacuate. Cheshire and Martin dropped their markers with deadly accuracy, and the rest of the squadron was then called in to bomb. The factory was totally destroyed and no one was killed. Not one bomb had missed.

This was the turning point. Cheshire had proved to all the sceptics that high level precision bombing was possible, providing the target was accurately marked from a low level. But Cheshire realised that even greater accuracy could be achieved using a smaller and faster aircraft, such as the Mosquito. Cheshire managed to convince AVM Cochrane, and the squadron received two Mosquitoes to practice with.

There were problems with high level precision bombing highlighted during this training period, and which we worked together to solve. For example, it was necessary to have a steady ten mile run up to the target, which was all very well over the practice range, but not when subjected to anti-aircraft fire. To combat this, the planes would circle outside the target area at predetermined different heights, and would approach the target from different directions. This should make it more difficult for enemy gunners to predict their fire on any one aircraft.

The squadron were now ready to try out the technique on a reasonably well defended target, which was to be a large aircraft factory near Toulouse. Cheshire dived low over the factory, but was not satisfied with his run and pulled away. Had he not been flying the Mosquito with its superior speed and handling qualities, he would have been hit by the heavy concentration of flak which opened up on him. He was satisfied with his third run, planted his markers, and the rest of us were called into bomb. The factory was totally destroyed. As a result of the operation's success, Cheshire received permission to increase the marking team, and received two more 'Mossies'. The idea was to train four pilots - Shannon and McCarthy, survivors of the 'Dam Raid', and Kearns and Fawkes - in low level marking, and then to detach 200 aircraft from the main force bombers to work with them to bomb specialised targets. Naturally, this caused friction between 617 Squadron and the Pathfinder Force, and relations remained strained for some time.

Amidst all this excitement, our crew members Bobby McCullough and Ronnie Pooley had reached the magical figure of thirty operations, and decided to call it a day. They felt that they had had a good run, and did not wish to push their luck any further. They were not to know at that moment that they had made the right decision. Had they carried on with the rest of us, they would have both been killed. We respected their decision, although we were sorry to see them go. Flying Officer Bill King joined us as flight engineer, and Flying Officer Ian Johnston took over Ronnie's guns in the mid upper turret. Both were very experienced officers, and it meant that the crew was mainly composed of officers, except for Sammy, Gerry and myself.

Our next target was to be the marshalling yards at Munich, an important rail centre in Germany. There was to be a raid at Karlsruhe to divert the enemy fighters away from the main target at Munich. Our crew was chosen to lead five other Lancasters on an additional spoof raid to Milan, using flares only. It proved to be an uneventful trip, highlighted only by the wonderful view as we flew over the Alps. The moonlight was reflected on the snow covered peaks, and Mount Blanc stood out supreme.

Meanwhile, everything was going according to plan. Karlsruhe had been bombed and had drawn the bulk of the night fighters. At Munich, the Mosquito marking force had dropped their markers on the railway lines, despite heavy anti aircraft fire. 5 Group bombers then dropped their bombs on the compact cluster of target indicators exactly as planned. Photographs showed that the marshalling yards had been totally destroyed.

Unfortunately, some of the markers had gone astray, and as a result some of the surrounding built up area suffered. As a result of this operation the 'Master Bomber' technique was evolved. This meant the leader remained in the area assessing and directing the pattern of bombing as the raid progressed, advising the crews over the radio telephone as to which clusters to aim for and which, if any, to ignore. The master bomber was in considerable danger of course, exposed to flak, searchlights and falling bombs for longer periods than most. Guy Gibson, the leader of the original dam raid, begged to be allowed back on operations as a master bomber, and was unfortunately killed in that role.

In mid May, 1944, we were told that all operations were suspended and we would be undergoing special training for a job of the utmost importance. The operation involved flying over water at predetermined heights, speeds and distances apart. In two waves of eight, sixteen planes would fly for thirty five seconds on one course, turn and follow a reverse course for thirty two seconds, before turning once again to its original course. The plane would therefore start the original heading slightly ahead of its last one and so on. This was to go on for eight hours, in two shifts.

There was a deathly hush followed by groans of protest. We surely had not been trained in precision bombing to finish up playing follow my leader over the sea at night! But after the initial shock had worn off we realised that there must be a good reason for it and we got down to the task in hand with as good a heart as we could find. Although precision flying was required, it was undoubtedly the most boring operation any of us had been called up to do, and we were soon all fed up to the back teeth.

In an effort to relieve the tension, Cheshire arranged a few diversionary exercises for us. One of them was a mini route march, but most of us disappeared into the nearest pub. It did give us all a much needed laugh, and even Cheshire saw the funny side of it. Another exercise was borrowed from the Commandos, and was intended to test our ingenuity should any of us be shot down. One Sunday morning, those crews involved had to report to the flight offices, empty their pockets of any money, and then were driven in blacked out vehicles into the middle of the countryside. The first crew back to Woodhall Spa would win a bottle of champagne. Some of the dedicated crews set off across the fields in an effort to be first back, whilst others thumbed lifts. One enterprising crew hitched a lift to a country pub which they frequented, persuaded the landlord to let them have drinks on the slate, and settled down for the night. A harassed landlord finally chucked them out after closing time, and they staggered back to camp in the early hours of the morning, very much the worse for wear. Cheshire may or may not have expected these exercises to be taken seriously, but they certainly did help to ease the tension, causing a laugh all round.

June 5th dawned, and suddenly everyone was confined to camp. We suspected that the long awaited invasion was about to take place. Once in the briefing room, we were told that the invasion was timed for the early hours of the following morning. Although the Allied Armies would be bearing the brunt of the invasion, we would have an important part to play. Now we would find out what lay behind the training we had been involved in.

The allied forces would be landing in different locations along the beaches of Normandy. The first few hours would be crucial, and it was of prime importance to keep the Germans guessing right up to the last minute as to the exact location of those landings. To achieve the element of surprise, a complicated deception plan had been worked out, and 617 Squadron were to play a vital role. It was code named 'Taxable', and the object was to give the impression that a large naval convoy was travelling across the channel to Calais, whilst the real invasion armada made its way to Normandy. Our practised flying patterns, plus the despatch of accurately weighed bundles of 'window' would give the impression on the German radar system of a full scale naval invasion fleet.

Once the object of the exercise had been explained to us, all our frustrations melted away. The first wave of planes took off at 23.00, each plane carrying additional men to despatch the bundles of 'window' precisely every fifteen seconds. The most difficult part of the operation, at least in training, had been when the second wave of aircraft relieved the first. It had to be done extremely smoothly so as not to cause interference to the picture that was, hopefully, unfolding on German radar screens. The operation demanded intense concentration and we were all shattered at the end. Apparently operation 'Taxable' achieved all that it set out to do, and the German armies around Calais were unable to move out in time to forestall the landings in Normandy.

Just after the D Day landings, the first consignment of Tall Boys arrived. At the same time we were informed that their big brother, 'Grand Slam' would soon be available too. This weighed an incredible 22000 lbs. It was hard to imagine flying with a bomb of that size suspended beneath you, and even harder to imagine landing with one on board. The ruling with regard to the Tall Boys was that if you could not positively identify the target you had to bring the bomb back, and we wondered if this policy would be reconsidered for the Grand Slam. We feared that the undercarriage would surely collapse under all that weight.

The Tall Boys were about to be tested on the Saumur Tunnel, near the River Loire. A German Panzer division was on its way to the coast to provide support to the German troops. They were travelling by rail and so it was essential to destroy the tunnel. Cheshire spotted the rails just before they disappeared into the tunnel mouth. He made his approach, diving to a low level, and

No Bacon and Eggs Tonight

released his target indicators. The rest of us then commenced the bombing. It was a pity that the first earthquake bombs of the war were falling on French soil. As they struck and corkscrewed their way into the earth, they gave a momentary flash. Photographs showed that there were huge craters around the tunnel mouth, with large sections of track ripped out altogether. One bomb had penetrated the hill beyond the tunnel mouth and bored its way into the tunnel itself before exploding. The earthquake effect caused the entire hillside to collapse inwards, as predicted, and the whole tunnel and surrounding lines were blocked for weeks. 617 were back with a big bang, and doing the job we had been trained to do.

We were soon given a new target. German E boats had been causing havoc amongst the allied shipping carrying reinforcements and supplies to the beachheads. (E boats were surface vessels as opposed to U boats which were submarines). The Allied Command decided to attack them as they prepared to leave on their nightly raids. Barnes Wallis believed that the earthquake effect over water would cause more damage than over land, and if the timing was right the fleet would be damaged by the resulting tidal wave. We were to drop the Tall Boys onto the concrete submarine pens. Again, the raid was successful with most, if not all, of the E boat fleet either sunk or rendered unseaworthy.

A similar raid was launched on Boulogne the following night. Cloudy conditions prevailed, and many crews had difficulty spotting the markers. Some did successfully bomb, but the rest of us had to return to Woodhall Spa, and according to the directive had to land with the Tall Boys on board, which turned out to be a very hairy experience indeed.

The day after the abortive Boulogne raid saw the start of the German missile offensive on London. Nobody, least of all the Germans, could predict where they would land. London however, is a vast city, and no matter where they landed they were bound to cause damage and loss of life. We were immediately briefed to attack one of these missile launching sites, Watten, in the Pas de Calais, France.

We had now started daylight operations which I personally did not like, and due to adverse weather conditions, we were stood around all day waiting for the signal to take off, fortified by coffee and sandwiches from the WAAFs. This went on for three days until the Met. Office announced that the weather had cleared over France. By this time everyone's temper and nerves were a tiny bit frayed. The poor armourers, however, were the worst affected by these on-off delays. Fearing that the weight of the bombs might cause permanent damage to the undercarriage of the Lancasters if they were left suspended for too long in the bomb bays, they had to unwinch them after each stand down was called.

Once over the missile launching target, Cheshire made his usual dive, but as it was daylight Cheshire had opted for smoke bombs as markers, and they failed to ignite. Luckily, Shannon had better luck, and the Tall Boys did their usual damage.

A similar attack was scheduled for a rocket launching site at Wizernes the following day, but again the weather had its say and we were unable to positively identify the target. Once again we had to land with the huge bombs on board. The continual pounding that these landings inflicted on the undercarriages were causing structural faults to appear, and the poor ground crews were hard pressed to repair them in time for the next operation.

There was another attack scheduled for the 22nd June, but yet again Mother Nature intervened and the bombs were brought back to base. We seemed to be fated with our attacks on these rocket sites, in conflict with the weather as much as the enemy.

And so it was that we arrived at the 24th June 1944, which as far as our own crew was concerned, turned out to be a day of destiny.

A photograph taken in 1982 of the dome of the V2 site at Wizernes.

The base was finally put out of action by 617 Squadron on their fourth attempt on the 17th July 1944.

13

JUNE 24TH DAY OF DESTINY

Briefing was over and we were standing around waiting for the trucks, having tea and sandwiches. We would have to wait until our return before enjoying our bacon and eggs. It was a glorious sunny afternoon with blue skies. As a result we were all wearing the minimum of flying clothing. I was wearing my battle dress blouse, gloves and flying boots, with my forage cap rolled up and fastened under the strap on the shoulder of my battle dress blouse. My warm roll necked pullover remained hanging in the locker, a mistake which I was soon to bitterly regret.

The crew was in reasonable spirits, although we were anxious to get this over and done with. This was the third time we had been bound for Wizernes, a V2 rocket site near to St Omer in the Pas de Calais area. I wondered what the reception would be like. By now, the Germans knew it was on our hit list and their deadly 88 mm anti aircraft guns would no doubt have been reinforced and be lying in wait for us.

We would be flying a different kite, because our own was US (unserviceable) due to the structural damage incurred when we had landed with the Tall Boy. No one liked to fly in a strange kite. Apart from the superstitious fears, there were the practicalities of familiarity. Just like a car, no two planes handled quite the same. On the way to the dispersal point, the butterflies in the stomach took over. No matter how many successful operations you had completed successfully, the fear remained.

Cheshire and Fawkes would again be using smoke bombs as markers. How I hated these daylight raids! As a result of daylight flying, we carried an extra gunner, Tom Price, to help combat the menace of German fighters. We paid particular attention to pre flight checks, on account of it being a strange aircraft, but soon were airborne, at which point I heaved my usual sigh of silent relief.

We set course for France, flying in two V formations of five aircraft, which Cheshire had christened a 'gaggle'. The planes flew about seventy yards apart, but at different heights. As we were flying in daylight I felt exposed and ill at ease.

We were approaching the target area at our predetermined height of 17000 feet and had just started on our long bombing run, flying straight and level, when ominous puffs of smoke appeared in the sky in front of us and much too close for comfort. My worst fears seemed to have come true and the enemy gunners seemed to have accurately predicted our height and range, and as a result were pumping shells into us from those dreaded 88 mm guns.

Before we could take any avoiding action we were hit in one of the port engines, followed immediately by another direct hit. I had a sickening feeling in the pit of my stomach. The unthinkable had happened. After all this time, and into our second tour of operations, our luck had finally run out. We had got the chop.

I glanced around and Bill King, our flight engineer was slumped to the floor. He had been hit by lumps of flying shrapnel and one glance was enough to tell me that he was dead. At least he did not suffer. By now the whole of the port wing was a blazing mass, and I knew instinctively that it was all over. There was no way back for us.

Suddenly, over the intercom came those dreaded words that we had been foolish enough to think that we would never hear. The prearranged code words "Abracadabra! Abracadabra! Jump! Jump!"

14

PRISONER

I quickly came back to reality, and realised that I had not been day dreaming. The stark reality was that we had been shot down. I glanced down and noticed that I was minus my flying boots. They were the loose fitting type, fur lined and which zipped up the front. Along with many other air crew, I had zipped them half way up the leg, and then turned them down, as the weather was particularly warm. The force of the air must have torn them off when I jumped out. For a moment a faint smile crossed my face as I thought how comical I must appear dangling in space in my stockinged feet, but it soon vanished as the full impact of the situation dawned on me. Below me, I saw two more 'chutes open, with one much lower than the other, and I heaved a sigh of relief, and said a silent prayer of thanks. At least three of us had managed to get out, and I began to wonder who else had made it apart from myself.

On nearing the ground I could see several grey uniformed figures running along the road in my general direction, obviously the reception committee. I was frightened to see them pointing their rifles at me as I neared the ground, and I actually feared they would fire at me. I landed in a field full of poppies, adjacent to the road along which the Germans were running. Amazingly, as I hit the ground, I remembered to bend my legs and roll over as per the drill, and at the same time I hit the quick release catch on my parachute harness, allowing the whole lot to fall away from me, with the parachute billowing gently in the breeze. No sooner had I disentangled myself and got to my feet, than the first of the soldiers

No Bacon and Eggs Tonight

arrived, waving his rifle around like somebody possessed, and puffing and panting into the bargain. Discretion being the better part of valour, I put up my hands as a token of surrender. There was no point in doing anything else as I had no chance of escape.

By now, the rest of the less fit reinforcements had arrived in an even worse state than their colleague. The first man on the scene took control and began to search me for hidden arms, whilst the remainder kept their rifles trained on me. My captors were well past their sell by date, and two of them were despatched to retrieve my parachute. They finally caught up with it, and bundled it up. Meanwhile, Captor Number 1, obviously satisfied that I was carrying no weapons started gesticulating to me to follow him down the road. He signalled to me to lower my arms which was a great relief and walked by my side. It was most uncomfortable in my socks, and I cursed my rotten luck in losing my boots. Somebody somewhere was going to find a good pair of boots at my expense!

We eventually reached the outskirts of a village, and crowds of curious French people were standing in groups until moved on by the guards. One elderly Frenchman however, managed to give me a V for victory sign, and I smiled back at him. At least I am supposing it was *that* V-sign - it could have been the other I suppose! Eventually we entered a building, presumably the local German Headquarters, where I was ushered into a room and my guard took up his position by the door. About an hour later the door opened and two soldiers carrying automatic weapons beckoned me to follow them. They led me into a large open car, and I was signalled to get in the back with one soldier on either side of me, their guns resting on their knees. A word of command was issued to the driver, and we set off. The journey was made in silence, and after some miles we came to the town of St. Omer.

The car stopped outside a large building sporting the Swastika flag, and I was made to follow them into the building. The place was full of soldiers and jackbooted officers, and civilian girls scurrying about, clutching files and documents as they went about

Prisoner

their business, apparently far too busy to notice an individual wearing a strange uniform and walking in his stockinged feet. I was taken to a small office containing a desk and two chairs only, and I was left in there with a guard posted outside. Shortly after, the door opened and a German officer entered. I stood to attention, whilst he himself sat down behind the desk. To my surprise he spoke English reasonably well. He asked me my number, rank and name and relieved me of my personal possessions, which he placed in a paper bag in his desk.

When the shell burst hit the plane, a piece of shrapnel must have penetrated my left buttock. It was not serious, but it had made a gash and I could feel the blood oozing around the wound. I mentioned this to the interrogator who said something to the guard in German. I was taken to a sickbay, but the doctor in attendance could not speak English. I pointed to my leg, and he nodded back to me, indicating to me to remove my trousers so that he could inspect the wound. At this point he made his exit, leaving me standing like an idiot with my trousers around my ankles! Fortunately, he quickly returned, with an interpreter. I was given a local anaesthetic, whilst the piece of shrapnel was removed, and a tetanus injection. He told me that the gash was about two inches long, and jokingly added that it was not serious enough to allow me to apply for repatriation. The wound was then stitched and dressed.

Feeling better for that, I dressed and the guard returned me to the interrogator. He asked me what target we had been attacking, and what squadron I was serving with. He sarcastically remarked that it must be a very poor Air Force if they did not provide their crews with flying boots. I refused to answer any more questions. He became angry, and as a punishment for my insolence, as he called it, I was made to stand face to the wall with my hands on my head.

After standing like that for almost thirty minutes, I was allowed to relax, and then I was summoned to go outside where I was bundled into another car, and transported to what I presume was the local 'nick'. At any rate, I was ushered into a cell, and the door

No Bacon and Eggs Tonight

was shut and locked behind me. There was a bed alongside one wall, and I lay down and began to take stock of the situation.

I felt relieved that I was alive and in one piece. I kept wondering who had managed to bale out besides myself, and if by a miracle anybody else had survived the holocaust. All my instincts told me that the Skipper would not be one of them. My last view of him, was of him struggling to keep the stricken Lancaster flying for those few extra seconds, in order to give us a chance of baling out. Being older than the rest of us, he had always exercised a lot of influence over the rest of the crew, and he was held in great respect by us all. I was going to miss him greatly.

I tried to delude myself into thinking that some of the lads might have baled out too low for me to see the parachutes open, or that they might have even survived the crash, but I knew in my heart of hearts that it was most unlikely. I also began to think of home, and I wondered how long it would be before they informed my mother that we had been reported as missing, and how she would react at the news.

Suddenly, the cell door opened and a jolly looking man, grinning all over his face, came in with a thick slice of bread, and some strange looking liquid which I later learnt was German coffee - or rather a war time version of it. I managed to convey to him the message that I needed to go to the toilet - no easy matter without being accused of breaking the Obscenity Act! Still grinning, he escorted me down the corridor to the toilet, and then back again to the cell.

Some time later he returned, and to my delight handed me a pair of flying boots! I tried to thank him, but he just shrugged his shoulders and continued to grin. I tried the boots on, and to my amazement I found that they fitted me perfectly. They were of a much better quality than my own had been, and I had not seen that style before. They were made in the form of a leather soled shoe with a soft fleecy lined top and zip fastener. On inspection it was

Prisoner

clear that they had been made in such a way that you could easily cut the soft leather tops away, and be left with a respectable pair of civilian walking shoes. They had obviously been made that way to assist the wearer should he ever be in a position to evade capture, or to make an escape attempt. It would certainly be less conspicuous than walking around in flying boots!

The Royal Air Force Benevolent Fund.
PATRON : H.M. THE KING.
PRESIDENT : H.R.H. THE DUCHESS OF KENT.
CHAIRMAN : THE RT. HON. LORD RIVERDALE, G.B.E.

Telephone No. : HOVE 3992.
All Communications to be addressed to the Secretary.

Our Reference MPM/AMS/218

EATON HOUSE,
14, EATON ROAD,
HOVE, SUSSEX.
12th July 1944

Mrs. E. M. Brook,
132 Duke Street,
Southport,
Lancs.

Dear Madam,

The Council of The Royal Air Force Benevolent Fund have learnt with much regret that your son is reported missing, and I am asked to express their very sincere sympathy.

I am to inform you that if your missing son was making you a voluntary allotment from his Royal Air Force pay, you will be entitled to continue cashing the orders in your Royal Air Force order book for a period. If, however, you do not receive a communication from the Air Ministry regarding your title to a temporary allowance within three weeks from the date of this letter you should communicate direct with the Director of Accounts, Air Ministry, (Accounts 7X.Cas)., Whittington Road, Worcester. If your son had not made you a voluntary allotment but was making you regular payments for your support through unofficial channels, you should inform the Director of Accounts to this effect without delay.

Should you be in need of some financial assistance either now or at any time in the future, kindly let me know and I will arrange for our Representative to interview you at the earliest opportunity.

Yours truly,

Squadron Leader,
Joint Secretary.

No Bacon and Eggs Tonight

As I sat on the bed I could see from the tiny window that it was growing dusk, and I suddenly realised that I was ravenous. Apart from the sandwiches and coffee we had had before take off, and the solitary piece of bread my gaoler had brought me, I had not had anything substantial since breakfast. Perhaps it was just as well that I did not know that it would be a long time indeed before I had a substantial meal again. The constant feeling of hunger was something that I was going to have to live with over the coming months.

I thought of the other crews who had flown with us today. God willing, they would all be back safely at Woodhall Spa. Debriefing would have been carried out, and everybody would have been asked to give their accounts as to our fate. The intelligence officers would be particularly interested in the amount of flak concentrations, and whether there had been any fighters around. The military police would have been around the billets and collected our personal items and kit. I knew the drill well enough, having witnessed it more than once on 50 Squadron.

The air crews would be putting on a brave face, but inwardly they would be feeling depressed. Losing a crew was always a dramatic experience for everybody including the ground crew, who not only lost the crew, but their beloved kite as well. The fact that the squadron had had a good run lately without any losses would not make them feel any better either, as the more superstitious would be wondering if our loss would herald a run of others. Fate did seem to play tricks like that, and I believe that most air crews were superstitious up to a point, even if they did not openly admit to it.

Still hungry of course, I thought of how the lads would have had their night flying supper by now, and would be relaxing in the mess, having a few pints, and getting one in for us, as was the custom. But for me, there would be no luxury of bacon and eggs tonight. I pulled the collar of my battle dress closer around my neck, and tried to make myself comfortable on the bed. I must have dozed

Prisoner

off, because it was quite dark when I awoke to the sound of heavy anti aircraft fire, and the thud of falling bombs. It suddenly dawned on me that I was caught up in one of our own raids. The noise was unbelievable, with the batteries sending shell after shell up. I could hear the droning of heavily laden bombers overhead, and I wondered if the main strike force were attacking the rocket site at Wizernes again. The pandemonium must have lasted for fifteen minutes or so, during which I learned what it was like to be on the receiving end of one of our raids. It was not a pleasant experience.

I was awakened the following morning by my guard, who was still grinning like a Cheshire Cat, despite the raid of the previous night, and after going for a walk down the corridor to the toilet, I received a piece of bread and a mug of their foul coffee. It must have been several hours later when the cell door opened, and I was signalled to follow the guard. I was ushered to a waiting lorry, and told to climb aboard. The guard was a mean looking character, and although he spoke no English, he made it quite clear by his gestures what would happen if I were to make a run for it! He need not have bothered because I realised that escape was out of the question in broad daylight.

A few minutes later a familiar figure appeared from another direction, whom I recognised as Pritch. We were delighted to see one another again, and as he clambered aboard, we naturally tried to converse. The guard promptly put a stop to that, and ran towards us brandishing his automatic rifle. For one awful moment, I thought he was going to hit us, but fortunately for us, he must have had second thoughts, and he backed off. He was joined by another guard, who climbed on board, and immediately sat on the tail board facing us, with his rifle across his knees. After a short journey, the lorry pulled up outside a hospital, and orderlies bearing two stretchers approached the lorry, and off loaded the stretchers onto the floor. To our surprise and joy, we could see that one of the stretchers contained Gerry Hobbs, resembling a mummy with bandages and splints on his arm and leg.

No Bacon and Eggs Tonight

Whilst the guards were busy signing for the wounded, Gerry did manage to tell us that he remembered struggling to bale out, before blacking out. When he regained consciousness, he was receiving first aid for a broken arm and leg and other injuries.

It was not until after the war that I got the full story from Gerry. Apparently, a French farmer named Andre Schamp from the St Omer district had witnessed the plane hit by gun fire, and watched it as it plunged earthwards in a ball of fire. Shortly before hitting the ground, it exploded in mid air, and burning wreckage was strewn over a wide area. At great personal risk he raced over to the wreckage, in spite of the exploding ammunition, to see what aid he could give.

Andre found the bodies of the Skipper, Sammy and Tom Price, the front gunner, in the wreckage. Ian Johnston was still alive when Andre pulled him clear of the scene, but was critically injured, and he died the next day in the hospital at St Omer.

After three trips to the Germans in Longuenesse to obtain the necessary permission, Schamp arranged for Teddy, Sammy and Tom to be buried alongside one another in the village church at Leulinghem. An inscription on the gravestone reads; "I will lift up mine eyes unto the hills from whence cometh my help". A month later, they found the body of Bill King, the flight engineer, in an adjoining field about two hundred yards away. Bill and Ian were buried at the War Graves Cemetery, Longuenesse, near to St Omer.

All the paper work completed, the guards once more took up their positions on the tail board, and once more we set off on our journey. The guards were still adopting a menacing attitude towards us, and I got the clear impression that given any provocation, they would not have hesitated in using their fire arms. We made sure we gave them no excuses, and remained silent for the duration of the journey. After a long drive, we eventually arrived on the outskirts of a large town, which we later discovered was Lille. We stopped outside a large hospital, where orderlies unloaded the stretchers and

Andre Schamp by the graves of the Skipper, Sammy and Tom in the village church at Leulinghem in the early 1980's.

carried them inside. The guards were watching us so closely, that we were not able to wish Gerry goodbye.

The final stop on our journey was a very foreboding building. You only had to look at the high stone walls and huge iron gates to know that this was the local gaol. The huge gates were opened to admit us, and we were ordered out of the truck at gun point. Immediately the guards separated Pritch and myself. The last I saw of him was being hustled through a door. We never met again, and eventually he was sent to an 'Oflag' or officers prison camp while I was sent to a camp for NCOs - a 'Stalag'. Pritch did survive the war, and at the end of hostilities returned home to Canada, but sadly died some years later.

I was escorted down a maze of passages by an elderly guard, whose one ambition seemed to be to deposit me in my cell as soon as possible. Outside the cell door he selected one key from a huge bunch, opened the door and locked me inside. The cell was dark, and it took a little while for my eyes to adjust to the gloom. I walked over to the rough wooden bed, and sat down on the edge, feeling miserable and lonely. The prospect of staying in this hole was depressing, and did nothing to raise my morale. I was feeling cold and ravenous, which was not surprising considering that I had not eaten since morning. I regretted bitterly not wearing my thick roll necked pullover, which was hanging back in my locker at Woodhall Spa.

Standing on the floor at the head of the bed was a bucket, which was obviously to be used as a latrine, and hanging from a nail on the wall was a toilet roll. It was all grim and unhygienic, but there was no point in complaining about it so I would have to make the best of it. Hopefully I would not be here too long. I must have dozed off for a while, for I was startled to hear the key turn in the lock, and then the door open. A different gaoler handed me a bowl of watery soup and a slice of bread. I sat down on the bed and gobbled every last crumb even though it tasted foul. By now it was getting quite dark, and pulling the collar of my battle dress tunic

Prisoner

closer around my ears, I tried to make myself as comfortable as possible.

The following morning I was awakened by brilliant sunshine through an iron grill high up on the wall above the end of the bed. The sight of the sunshine cheered me up no end and although I was still hungry I felt in a better frame of mind.

I took a closer look at my surroundings and was still not impressed. It reminded me of the cells as depicted in the pre-war movie "The Tale of Two Cities". The only thing missing was the ball and chain stapled to the wall and the old bedraggled prisoner with his beard down to his knees. The solid door appeared to be made of oak, and it was reinforced with big iron bands. In the centre of the door a peephole had been cut to allow the gaoler to keep the occupant under observation. The walls were made of thick blocks of stone and must have been one foot thick. The cell measured approximately ten feet by six. The bed was against one wall, but there was no mattress or blanket.

Although I am only small, I found that by standing on the bed I could spring up and grab the bars, haul myself up and look out of the grille. My cell overlooked the courtyard and prisoners, some in uniform and some in civilian clothes, were taking exercise under the watchful eye of the armed guards. The strain on my arms proved too great, and I had to let go, collapsing onto the bed. I came to the conclusion that this was a civilian prison, and I wondered if the inmates were political prisoners, and what they had done, to deserve being shut up in a hole like this. I noticed several names and dates scratched on the wall, and under the names were scratched figure ones, obviously representing the number of days that they had occupied the cell. The length of stay seemed to vary between four and eight days. Most of the names were British, but there were French names too, and I began to wonder if this wing of the gaol was serving as a holding gaol for Allied Prisoners. Some of the inmates had written RAF or ARMY alongside their names. I decided to add

No Bacon and Eggs Tonight

my name to those already there but I could find nothing suitable to use as a tool.

But then I remembered the toy mascot dog I had fastened to the lapel of my battle dress blouse with a safety pin. This had been given to me by my sister as a lucky mascot when I joined 50 Squadron prior to starting my operational flying. I was very surprised that the German Luftwaffe had not confiscated it along with everything else but luckily for me they had overlooked it. With the aid of the safety pin, I managed to scratch my name on a blank piece of wall, and underneath I added the figure one, representing my first night behind bars in this cell. It was tedious work, but at least it gave me something to occupy my mind.

I thought I heard a clock chiming, and listened carefully for the time. I heard it strike six o'clock, and shortly afterwards I heard the guard's footsteps. The key grated in the lock and the door opened. I was confronted by a new guard, and he thrust a broom into my hands indicating that I should sweep out the cell. That small chore having apparently been completed to the guard's satisfaction, he escorted me to a small wash room containing a grubby toilet, where I was to empty the contents of the bucket. I was allowed a quick swill under the cold water tap but had to dry myself on my handkerchief, which was none too clean by now. In fact, it was on a par with my own state of cleanliness. I trudged back reluctantly, feeling dirty and dishevelled, and once installed, the guard slammed the door and relocked it.

At seven, the usual breakfast of coarse brown bread and coffee was served. I devoured it greedily and even though it tasted like sawdust, it was welcome just the same.

I decided to take another look outside, so leaping up from the bed and gripping the bars, I hauled myself up once more and peered out of the grille. The prisoners were walking around in single file, looking utterly dejected. The scene depressed me so much, that

I vowed not to look out again, and flopped back on to the bed, wondering if I would be joining them outside in the courtyard.

I realised that to prevent becoming too despondent, I would have to keep as active as possible, but my options were limited, being confined to a tiny cell. I decided on two PT sessions morning and afternoon, coupled with walkabouts around the cell, and then periods of rest. This way I hoped to keep body and mind active, and make me sufficiently tired to enable me to sleep better at nights.

I was still wondering when I would be on my way to the Interrogation Centre at Frankfurt, Germany, known to we airmen as 'Dulag Luft'. Looking at the dates on the wall the longest stay appeared to be about one week, but of course all this was speculation. I set about my exercises with enthusiasm, but despite all my good intentions time continued to drag and I never lost the feeling of hunger. I found myself waiting for the clock to chime to relieve the boredom, and I even looked forward to sweeping the cell out and my daily visit to the wash room to 'slop out'.

On the 29th June, a guard escorted me down the corridors to a large room, where to my surprise I found about twenty other Allied Airmen, all of us NCOs. We were led one by one to tables, behind which were sat German Luftwaffe NCOs. All our documents were on the tables before them. We were scrutinised and searched before being formed into two ranks, and then marched out through the gates and into the world beyond.

We arrived at a railway siding where we were instructed to climb on board a train, with about ten of us to each compartment. We were soon chatting to one another, and naturally the topic of conversation focused on each other's experiences, leading up to our being shot down, and since our capture. The chatter got so loud, that the guards who up until that point had kept a very low profile, came dashing in to see what was going on, and made it clear that we were to shut up. Suitably admonished, we toned it down somewhat, and tried to relax in our cramped quarters.

At long last, the train got under way. We left Lille behind us, and soon were travelling through the rolling country side. At this stage, we were not sure where our destination lay, but we were all of the opinion that it would be Dulag Luft at Frankfurt. This was the interrogation centre, to which all Allied Airmen were sent prior to going to a permanent PoW camp.

Prior to "D" day, part of the Allied bombing offensive had been diverted away from the German cities to attacking oil supply targets, and the railway network, in Belgium, France and of course Germany itself. The result of this was the devastation of the railway network in Western Europe. Although we started at a brisk speed, the evidence of the damage inflicted on the rail system soon became apparent. Progress became very slow, and for long periods we did not move at all, and even when we did get underway, we would very soon be shunted off the main line, to allow the passage of troop or ammunition trains which were on their way to the battle area in Normandy.

As we drew ever nearer to Germany, the guards became more and more agitated. Up to now they had not bothered us too much, keeping to their compartments and only making the occasional sortie down the corridor to make sure that we were all there. But now they were dashing into the compartments to pull the blinds down, and indicating that in no way were we to look out of the windows, or we would be shot. Naturally this strange behaviour only served to make us more curious.

We had worked out that our route was taking us South of the main Ruhr Valley towns and cities - our dreaded Happy Valley. Despite the heavy loses suffered by Bomber Command during the sustained Battle of the Ruhr, widespread damage had been inflicted on almost every town and city in the Ruhr Valley, so I suppose that it was only to be expected that the Germans would be very touchy and want to conceal the extent of the damage to the outside world - and us in particular.

Prisoner

One man sitting next to the window, was able to catch a glimpse outside as the blinds moved with the vibration of the train, and he gave us a running commentary about conditions outside. At one point he told us that we were travelling through Aachen, or at least what remained of it. Apparently he had caught a glimpse of the sign as we crept through the station. The train had by now ground to a halt again and most of us managed a crafty look outside when the guard was not looking. I do not think any of us were prepared for what we saw. The devastation was incredible. There were piles of rubble as far as the eye could see, and gaunt empty shells which had once been buildings. It was total destruction, and I can only liken it to the pictures of Hiroshima after the dropping of the atomic bomb.

It was not surprising that the guards were hopping about like demented dervishes. Naturally they did not want us to witness the devastation that we had inflicted on their cities, and I am quite sure that they would have shot us at the least provocation. The result was that we were particularly careful not to antagonise them in any way. They were of middle age, and for various reasons were no longer front line troops, but that did not make them less likely to exact vengeance on us, if we gave them any cause.

After an uncomfortable night with only water to drink, eventually we pulled into another siding which turned out to be our journey's end. Once on the platform, we were immediately formed up in two ranks and once more counted. We were most surprised to see a further dozen guards formed up on the platform. We could not understand why our small party warranted so many of them. Including the four that travelled with us it worked out at almost one guard per prisoner. I found it hard to believe that they thought we might try to escape in broad daylight, in the heart of Germany. Whatever the reason, they all formed a double guard on either side of us, and we started to march out of the siding, and into the built up area.

I soon realised the reason for the extra guards. It was not because they were afraid that some of us might attempt to run for it, but to protect us from the German civilians. There were not many of them thank goodness, because it was still early morning but they demonstrated their hostility in no uncertain manner. They walked along side the column, booing and waving their clenched fists at us. One man ran his finger over his throat, demonstrating only too clearly what our fate would have been had he been able to get at us.

Of course it was not surprising really, in view of the pounding they had received from both Bomber Command and the American Air Force prior to the invasion. It was no secret back home that Air Chief Marshall Harris, Commander in Chief of Bomber Command was itching to resume attacks on German cities and towns, still believing in his ability to force Germany to surrender by bombing alone. I don't think that there were too many who still shared his views however. At least for the moment the cities were getting a slight respite from attack.

The threatening crowd continued to walk with us, gesticulating, hissing and booing and for once I was relieved to see so many escorting guards. We would not have stood a chance if the crowd could have got at us. Fortunately one by one they gave up, and turned back still mouthing and shaking their fists, and I for one was relieved to see the back of them. We heard months later, that some American airmen who had baled out and landed in Frankfurt during a daylight raid had been caught by civilians and hung on the spot. This was only hearsay but I have no doubt in my mind that that would have been their fate. Alone at last, we continued on our way until we saw in the distance the gates leading to the camp.

15

OBERURSEL INTERROGATION CENTRE

The guards, having completed their task of escorting us from the siding to the Interrogation Centre, picked up their automatic weapons and prepared to leave. I can honestly say that was the only time I was pleased to see so many guards around me. Being exposed to all those hostile civilians on the march from Frankfurt siding to the centre was a most frightening experience, and one which I would not wish to undergo again.

The German administration staff at Oberursel or Dulag Luft as we prisoners knew it, had received plenty of experience over the years in admitting Allied airmen to the centre for interrogation, and the arrival of our small intake of prisoners provided no problem at all for their well oiled machine. One by one, we were vetted and documented with the utmost speed, and the minimum of fuss. Photographs, both frontal and profile, were taken, as were fingerprints. Our height and weight were also recorded, together with our service number, rank and name. I was then escorted to my cell.

I sat on the bed to take stock of my surroundings. The cell was much the same as Lille in terms of size. There was a wooden framed bunk between the door entrance and the cell wall. The base of the bunk was made of wooden slats going across, but they were all of different thicknesses, making it extremely uncomfortable to lie down on. I wondered if that was by accident or design, and decided that it was probably the latter. There was no mattress or blanket available so that meant I would have to sleep on the uneven boards or even on the floor.

There was a space of almost four feet from the end of the bunk to the outside wall opposite the door. At the top of this wall, was a grille about two foot square with iron bars going across. There appeared to be shutters outside which could be closed if necessary. Because the end of the bunk was so far from the wall, I was unable to spring up and grab the bars to look outside. The walls were plastered unlike Lille, but names and dates had been scratched on them in just the same way.

There was no bucket, so I assumed that toilet facilities would be available. By operating a lever in the cell, a signal arm would raise on the outside of the door, indicating that the inmate required attention.

I remembered our limited training about the type of methods the Germans might employ to gain information, such as the use of secret microphones. The Germans had also been known to plant a stooge in an adjoining cell with particularly thin walls with a view of engaging the prisoner in conversation, again hoping that in an unguarded moment the prisoner might let something slip which would prove important to their intelligence. Then there was the bogus Red Cross representative, who full of charm and promising to do everything to help you, would try to induce you to complete a questionnaire.

Left to my own devices, I went over the cell with a fine toothed comb. Having decided that the cell was free of microphones I settled down on the bunk but without much success. The uneven boards cut into my back and caused great discomfort. Whilst I lay, tossing from side to side, I heard two lots of foot steps coming down the corridor, eventually stopping outside my door.

A tall man dressed in civilian clothes entered the cell. On his arm he wore the familiar Red Cross emblem. He introduced

Oberursel Interrogation Centre

himself as a Swedish representative of the Red Cross, and that he was here to see that I received fair treatment, and that he would do everything possible to make my stay as tolerable as possible under the circumstances. He asked permission to sit down on the bunk, and put his brief case alongside him. He chatted about this and that before opening his case and taking out a form. So far things were turning out as predicted, and I smiled to myself as I wondered what his next move would be.

I decided to go along with him for a while to see how far he would go with his charade. I told him that I had been slightly wounded, and had been treated by a German doctor, but had received no dressing since then. He immediately operated the lever, which in turn dropped the signal arm outside with a great clatter. The guard opened the door and after a few brief words in German, departed to reappear some minutes later together with an orderly complete with white coat and first aid box. He inspected the wound, nodded his head in approval, and changed the dressing. I must admit that I felt much better for it.

My benefactor continued to sympathise with me for being here and hoped that I would soon be on my way to join my colleagues at a permanent PoW camp. He did not seem to be in any hurry to get to the point, and I was beginning to think that I may have misjudged him after all when he suddenly handed the questionnaire to me. He suggested that I should read it through before answering the questions, and sign at the bottom. I glanced at it, and although it started off innocently enough, it was clear that if I were to answer all the questions I would finish up back in prison when the war was over! I completed only the section that asked for my number, rank and name. I smiled to myself at the look of injured innocence on his face, but he had not finished yet.

He asked me if I was aware that in retaliation to the terror bombing of German Cities by the RAF and the American Air Forces, the German government had decreed that all Allied airmen may be treated as terrorists, and would not be protected by the

Geneva Convention. He also added that it was at the discretion of the Luftwaffe here at Dulag Luft whether we would be considered as prisoners of war, or whether we would be handed over to the civilian courts, who would try us as terrorists. He strongly advised me to consider my position carefully, but he assured me that the Luftwaffe authorities would deal sympathetically with any prisoner who co-operated with them. He also pointed out to me, that if I did not complete the form, I would be registered as missing presumed killed, and he reminded me of the effect that would have on my family back home. With that thought ringing in my mind, he replaced the form in his brief case, summoned the guard and departed.

I wondered if I would see him again, but I doubted it. I lay back on the bunk smirking, and congratulating myself that I handled myself well, and that round one belonged to me. Perhaps it was just as well that I did not know that there were many rounds to go yet, before I finally put Dulag Luft behind me, otherwise I would not have been feeling so self satisfied.

Later that evening, my cell door opened, and I was told to stand on the threshold by an English speaking guard. A trolley was standing outside, and I was handed a slice of bread and mug of coffee. I glanced down the corridor to see if I could see any fellow sufferers, but there was no one in sight. I was then pushed back into my cell and locked in.

Sometime later nature called, so I operated the lever. When the guard finally arrived, I was grateful to be able to speak to him in English. We walked down the corridor to the wash room at the end and I was pleasantly surprised to see that it was a vast improvement on the gaol at Lille. I asked permission to wash, but was only allowed to swill my hands and dry them on a roller towel. There was nothing to do to pass the time, not even a clock chiming, but I did hear prisoners operating their signal arms from time to time, and the tramping of feet up and down the corridor. This provided some comfort to me, knowing that I was not completely on my own, and that there were other prisoners in the same boat as me.

Being the end of June, the daylight was at its longest period, and although I had no watch or clock I had a good idea of the time. As soon as dusk fell, the single bulb protected in the ceiling by a metal cage was switched on, but it never occurred to me that it would remain on all night long. As I lay on my bed, trying desperately to get into a more comfortable position, a large pole with a hook on the end appeared outside the grille and the shutters were placed into position outside, leaving just the narrowest of gaps to allow for ventilation. At the same time I noticed a distinct rise in the temperature. One would have expected the temperature to get cooler as the sun went down.

I got up from the bed, and soon realised that a pipe on the same wall as the grille, presumably a heating pipe, was hot to the touch. I tried to settle down once more, making a pillow out of my battle dress blouse, but without much success, as no matter how I twisted and turned, the uneven boards continued to dig into my back. Furthermore, I could not escape from the glare of the light which was shining directly into my eyes. I changed positions continually, but it made no difference at all.

The cell door then opened, and the guard instructed me to hand over my boots, which he stood in the corridor outside my door. I just had time to catch a glimpse of rows of boots lined in the corridor before he pushed me roughly inside, before relocking the door. It reminded me of putting your shoes outside the bedroom door in a hotel ready for the boot boy, but of course this was no hotel, and we inmates were not scheduled for five star treatment.

I clambered back onto the bed, and tried once more to settle down. I prayed that they would turn the light off, but they did no such thing, neither did they turn off the heat. It was like being in an oven, and most uncomfortable.

No Bacon and Eggs Tonight

And so it was that somehow I got through the first of many sleepless nights at Dulag Luft. Already I was beginning to discover how tough solitary confinement can be, especially when you are deprived of sleep, and only given enough food to keep you alive. I must have dozed off at some point during that first night, but was brought back to life with the noise of the shutters being opened, and the brilliant flooding of light through the grille. I ached in every limb as I rose from the bed. Shortly afterwards, the ceiling light was switched off, and when I bent down to feel the central heating pipes, they were barely warm to the touch.

The guard then returned my boots, still with all the mud intact. The food trolley was outside, and I was handed the usual slice of bread, and mug of coffee. I sat back on the bed, and devoured my meagre breakfast in no time at all. I found that I was gradually getting used to the coarse texture of the bread, and the sour taste that it left in your mouth. Despite the shortcomings, it was the only food we were going to receive, and at least it served to ease the aching void in my stomach.

After my lunch of watery soup and bread, I was escorted to my first interrogation. We returned to the admin. block, passing dozens of people, male and female including civilians, all dashing about clutching files and pieces of paper in their hands. At last we stopped outside a particular door. A voice from within and speaking fluent English, bid us to come in. A middle-aged man in the military uniform of the Luftwaffe, was sat behind a large desk. At last he looked up, and asked me why I had not completed the form given to me by the Red Cross representative. Did I not realise that the form was designed to separate the genuine cases from the terrorist flyers? In his experience, the only airmen who refused to complete the form, were those who had something to hide. I replied by giving my number, rank and name only.

He echoed what the 'Red Cross' man had said in that all Allied air men were to be treated as terrorists. He then asked me if I fully realised the seriousness of my position. The Luftwaffe were under great pressure to hand the likes of me over to the civilian authorities, so that we could be tried in a civilian court. He hoped that I would understand the implications of that. If I were found guilty, I could receive the death sentence, or at the very least a long sentence in a labour camp. On the other hand, if I were to show some sort of remorse, and co-operate with him, he could still help me. He went on to say, that I had forfeited the right to be treated as a PoW by adopting this stubborn attitude.

After this outburst, his mood softened, and he became more conciliatory towards me. He adopted a fatherly attitude saying that he wanted to help me join my friends and fellow countrymen at a PoW camp. On that note, he brought the interview to an end, except to say that he would see me again in a few days time, after I'd taken time out to consider his remarks. I must admit that I had been shaken by his outburst, but was still convinced that he was bluffing. I assumed that once he realised he was getting nowhere with me, he would ship me off to a PoW camp. This was another example of me underestimating the determination of the Germans to pursue everything to the bitter end.

Back in my cell, I added my name to the already large list of names scratched on the wall. It was the 1st July, and with the aid of my pin, I scratched my name and the two lines representing the number of days I had been at Dulag Luft. I felt warm and uncomfortable, and on bending down to feel the pipes found them to be quite hot again. This did not surprise me in the least.

In fact, conditions were a repeat of the previous night, except for one additional trick that they had up their sleeves. In an attempt to get some sleep, I had decided to try and sleep on the floor, and at some point during the night I must have dozed off only to be suddenly awakened by the guard bursting into the cell, shouting for me to give my number, rank and name. At the same time he roughly hauled me to my feet, banging my head on the bed as he did so. He told me that I was not allowed to sleep on the floor, and from now on I would be kept under close scrutiny. He added that as apparently

No Bacon and Eggs Tonight

I was fond of answering all questions put to me by quoting my number, rank and name, from now on I would be asked to repeat it day and night, until I was sick and tired of doing it. That signalled the end of any rest I may have got. I cursed both the interrogator and the guard for disturbing me when I had managed to doze off.

The days and nights seemed longer than ever, and although I had resumed my exercises, my heart was not really in it and I just could not enter into the spirit of the thing. I realised that my condition was getting worse, and I could not forget the words of warning from the interrogator. I was beginning to dread the next interview, and wondered why he was not sending for me.

It was the 5th of July when the guard came for me and escorted me to the interrogator's office. To my surprise he was quite affable and handed me a cigarette, and offered to light it for me. He even apologised for only having German cigarettes, which he admitted were inferior to American and English ones. He was in a totally different mood from our last encounter, and was most pleasant and talkative. He went on to tell me that he had spent a lot of time in Britain as a boy, and that over the years, had grown to like and respect the British. He added that we were of similar character and temperament as the German race, and that it was tragic that we should find ourselves on opposite sides.

I wondered when he was going to stop singing our praises, and start the interrogation. I need not have worried. Almost as though he'd read my mind, he suddenly asked me if I had thought over his advice since our last meeting, and was I ready to co-operate fully with him? He leaned back in his chair as if he already knew what my answer would be. He added that I belonged to a squadron which had been engaged on specific terror raids against the German people, and that the civilian government were pressing him hard to hand me over to them. No longer feeling sure of my position, I said that under the Geneva Charter I could not say anything other than my number, rank and name, of which he was aware. Furthermore, I added, despite what he said, I was a member of an air crew who were engaged on legitimate targets, and as such, could not be handed over to a civilian court, but was under the protection of the Luftwaffe. I added that he had no right to threaten me with reprisals. And with that, I leaned back in my chair and took a long and deep drag from my cigarette, in an effort to control my nerves.

His face changed hue, and I thought he was going to burst a blood vessel. He stood up from his chair, his face distorted with anger. He leant across the desk, calling me arrogant and stupid, and knocked the cigarette out of my mouth. Still continuing his verbal assault on me as he ordered me to my feet, he made me retrieve the cigarette and stub it out on his ashtray. For my indiscretion, I was made to stand to attention for the remainder of the interview. He asked me what type of operations we were involved in, and how long we had been flying daylight raids. When I still refused to answer him, his anger flared again and he told me that he was fast losing his patience with me, and that he would see to it personally that I was locked up in solitary for the duration of the war, or until he was forced to hand me over to the civilian authorities. I could expect a very different type of interrogation then, he warned, but the Luftwaffe would then be powerless to intervene on my behalf. He had shown great patience and understanding with me, and this was how I repaid him?

Continuing his threats, he rang for the guard, who escorted me back to my cell. As the door slammed behind me I collapsed on the bed shaking like a leaf, torn between my loyalty to my country on the one hand and my sense of self preservation on the other. My mind was in a turmoil and I was unable to reason things out any more. I blamed myself for not showing more restraint at the interview. My little outburst was not going to do my cause any good. Worst of all I found that I was beginning to think that perhaps he was right, and that I deserved to be handed over to the Gestapo. Perhaps I was too stupid to realise that he was trying to help me. As I lay back on my bed, hungry, tired out through lack of sleep and my mind tormented by worry, I remembered how I had been proud of my tactical success over the bogus Red Cross man. I was now beginning to have serious doubts as to the wisdom of continuing this defiant stand against the inquisitor. Feeling alone and without friends, I wondered where it would all end.

How I managed to survive the next 5 days I shall never know, as I was by now in a very poor state mentally and physically. Never a night went by without them bursting into my cell at all hours demanding my number, rank and name. They had promised me that I would be sick of repeating it, and I was certainly being punished. I was sent for again on the 10th of July and once more I was subjected to threats, and then promises of leniency. There were more questions on our role on the eve of the invasion, and since the D day landings. He also seemed to have suddenly become interested in the type of bomb load we were carrying at the time of our being shot down. I was staggered at the apparent extent of his knowledge, but my answers followed the same pattern as on previous interrogations, but with much less conviction. Again he issued dire warnings and threats before ringing for the guard to take me back.

Back in my cell, physically sick and mentally drained, I began to realise I had almost reached the end of my tether. In my present state of mind I could no longer think logically and I was at the stage when I almost believed him when he kept telling me that I had forfeited all rights to be treated as a PoW, and that it was all my own fault.

I remained in this state of confusion where I was alternately blaming myself, and then the interrogator, for finding myself in this desperate situation. My next interrogation was on the 13 of July, and started where the previous one left off. He told me at I had reached the end of the line, and that he could not help me any further. With those remarks ringing in my ears, he rang the bell and an ominous looking character in civilian clothes came in. He sat down alongside the interrogator but never spoke a word during the remainder of the interview.

Oberursel Interrogation Centre

Finally the interrogator told me that he was sending me back to the cell, where I could ponder on things, and that he would call me in one hour's time.

I sat on the edge of the bed, with my head in my hands, feeling utterly dejected and terrified. I think this was one of the worst moments during the whole of my captivity. Frightened and bewildered as I was, I did manage to come to a decision. In no way was I going to be handed over to the civilian authorities. I was an airman, and as such was subject to the protection of the Luftwaffe. I would complete the form that seemed so important to them, and tell them anything they wanted to know although they seemed to know more than me anyway. I was not going to be a martyr or a hero either, and what I did not know I would make up. I had resisted the pressures as long as I could, but I could not take any more of it.

I heard the footsteps coming down the corridor, and I knew that they would stop outside my door. Once more I made the long trek down the corridor to the office and to my tormentor. The two men were sat at the desk as I walked in. I was asked what decision I had come to. My mouth was dry and I could hardly get a word out, although I had rehearsed them enough, but in that vital instant something told me to bluff it out a little longer.

With great difficulty, I repeated that I was an airman, and not a terrorist and that I was merely acting within my rights. There was a pause which seemed like an eternity, when to my amazement, the interrogator told me that he was terminating the interrogations. I still was not sure what he meant, assuming that he was going to hand me over to the Gestapo.

He continued to tell me that in the morning I would leave with some of my colleagues, for a transit camp at Wetzler prior to being moved to a permanent PoW camp. Noticing the look of astonishment on my face, he told me that he knew from the start that I had been a member of 617 Squadron, and that Wing Commander Gibson was the commanding officer. Whether that was a deliberate

No Bacon and Eggs Tonight

mistake on his part, I shall never know, but I did not enlighten him to the fact that Wing Commander Cheshire was now in command. He picked up a file from his desk, and told me that I would be surprised at the amount of information he had on our squadron.

I asked him if he knew so much, why had he kept me here so long and subjected me to this sort of treatment? His reply was that any piece of information that he gleaned from interrogations formed another piece in the giant jigsaw puzzle which he and his fellow intelligence officers were trying to solve. In my particular case, he had been able to find those scraps of information from another source, so there was no point in holding me any longer. He added that I should be under no illusions. He would have kept me in solitary confinement for as long as he thought that I could be of some use to him. With that he rang the bell and called the guard.

As a parting shot, he said that there was nothing personal in his method of interrogation, and he hoped I bore no grudges. There did not seem any point in replying to that, and with that, the guard took me back to the cell. I was still in a daze when the cell door clanged behind me. I collapsed on the bed, and burst into tears. I suppose it was relief that my ordeal was finally over, but whatever the reason, I felt no sense of shame.

I gradually recovered my composure, and tried to put into perspective what had happened. The interrogator would never know how close he came to completely breaking my resolve. They say that a human being can only cope with so much stress, be it physical or mental, and I had certainly reached my limit. It was as if a huge burden had been lifted from my shoulders, and for the first time in weeks I felt as though I could relax. I heard the guard's footsteps as he came down the corridor, and my heart missed a beat when he stopped outside my door. For one awful moment I thought that my tormentor had changed his mind and I was expecting the worst when he opened my cell door. But to my surprise he was smiling, as he asked me if I would like a wash and a shave. I did not need asking twice, and I followed him down to the wash room, where I stripped down to my underpants. He handed me a piece of soap, towel and razor. The water was not very hot and the blade non too sharp, but it was heaven just the same to be able to have my first proper wash and shave since I was shot down.

I felt like a new man, and there was even a spring in my step as I returned to the cell. On the way he asked me if I would like to read a book during my last night at Dulag Luft, and he promised to bring me one shortly. True to his word he returned in a few minutes with one, but better than that he produced a blanket as well. This was luxury, and I was able to fold it and lay it over the uneven boards. I lay down and started to read, feeling refreshed for the first time. As the light faded, the cell light was switched on and I was able to continue my reading. It was the sound of the guard closing the shutters that made me realise that it must be getting late, but tonight he passed me by. I bent down and felt the pipes, but they were quite cold. The guard escorted me to the toilet, but on my return he did not ask me to surrender my boots. Shortly after, the cell light went out and I was able to stretch out in reasonable comfort for the first time. I slept well, and no one burst into my cell to ask my number, rank or name. All that was behind me, thank goodness.

I wondered where Pritch was now, and if he too had been subjected to similar treatment. Strange as it may seem, his name was never once mentioned to me during any of the interrogations. Hopefully, I thought, Gerry would be languishing in a prison hospital and well out of it.

What did I learn from my experiences at Dulag Luft? One thing was clear, you could not beat the system. If they wanted to know something of importance to them from any prisoner, they would get that information from you one way or another in time. They held all the aces in the pack, and providing they had sufficient time to keep you locked up, they would win in the end. Apart from the one instance when the interrogator knocked the cigarette out of my mouth, there was never any threat of violence, but then they did not have to use any. Their method was to lower your powers of resistance systematically, by not allowing you to wash, a near starvation diet, interrupting what little sleep you could get, and above all isolation. Once you had been softened up sufficiently so that you could no longer think logically, then they had almost won.

Generally speaking, most airmen were only at Dulag Luft a couple of days, and their interrogation more of a formality. I have often wondered why I came in for their special attention. After all I was only a small cog in a large wheel and there was very little I could have told them anyway. The conclusion I finally came to was that he obviously knew that I was a member of 617 Squadron, and we happened to be the first crew from 617 to be shot down since D day.

I also believe that he was suspicious that we had been involved in the spoof raid that we carried out on the eve of the landings, when we dropped bundles of window to confuse the German Radar as to where the actual landings were to be, and wanted desperately to learn more about it. I also think that he was hoping that I could give him some information about the Tall Boy bomb which we had been carrying when we were shot down. In my particular case I was lucky that he gained sufficient information from other sources, otherwise I think I might have been the occupant of that cell for a long time.

As to my own reactions to that miserable period, I was extremely self critical of the way that I coped during my confinement at Dulag Luft. I was shocked with myself for even thinking of collaborating with the Germans in order to save myself from being handed over to the civilian courts, and I blamed myself for not realising that he was bluffing all the time. Or was he? The German Armed Services were coming under increasing pressure from Berlin to tighten security with regard to PoWs, so it is quite possible that prisoners might have been handed over to the Gestapo.

As time went by, and I drifted into life as a PoW, I found that I could begin to talk much more freely about my time in the interrogation centre, without the terrible feeling of guilt, which I had experienced immediately after it was all over, and without breaking into a cold sweat every time I relived those 13 days in solitary confinement. I have spoken to many people since the war who underwent similar experiences, and I have come to realise that my behaviour was in no way unique. In fact my reactions were what might be expected from somebody who had been subjected to long periods of stress. I had been reduced to that state by men specially trained in the art of psychological warfare and interrogation, and only the very strongest of personalities and wills could withstand that treatment for long.

Maybe if I had received more counselling and advice on how best to combat these interrogations from our own intelligence officers back home during our training, then maybe I and a lot more like me may have been able to cope a lot better. In some ways I felt badly let down by the RAF. It could be argued I suppose that the RAF just didn't have the time to give all Air Crew an intensive course on how to combat long periods of interrogation and solitary confinement, or even if the facts really justified it. After all it has to be admitted that most Air Crew were only in the centre for a day or two before being moved on to a permanent camp. But for the cases such as myself, I would have welcomed an inkling as to what I might have to endure. Most of us were very young men, little more than boys, and to suddenly find yourself in a situation over which you had no control and no idea of how to handle it, was a frightening experience.

Personally I think that the RAF in their wisdom had realised that if they placed too much emphasis on that aspect, then they might have frightened off a lot of trainee Air Crew, who were all volunteers anyway. They may have even been faced with a shortage of replacements to fill the gaps caused by the huge losses sustained by Bomber Command.

Long after the war was over, I read accounts in books of the methods employed by British interrogators in their dealing with

German prisoners of war, and was greatly surprised to see that their methods were almost carbon copies of the German methods, relying on the same recipe of deprivation, humiliation, lack of sleep and so on. The only difference seemed to be that the German prisoners received better food rations than we did. However, it does explain to some degree the decision by the RAF not to discuss the methods of German interrogators with us, and to even play it down, because I am sure that they would have been most reluctant to admit that that sort of treatment existed on both sides.

16

STALAG LUFT 7 - BANKAU

We left the interrogation centre on July 14th bound for the transit camp at Wetzler. Three days later a party of approximately forty airmen including myself were taken by train to our permanent PoW camp. We had been told that we were going to a new camp at Bankau, a mere spot on the map to us, situated east of Breslau in the province of upper Silesia, and almost on the Polish border. After two miserable days on the train when we were once more subjected to endless shuntings into the sidings, and with very little to eat, we pulled up on the morning of July 20th at a small railway halt which was apparently Bankau.

We were made to disembark, and after all the carriages had been searched to make sure that no prisoner had spirited himself away, the train was allowed to slowly steam away into the distance. After a head count, we were marched off down a very narrow country lane. It was very desolate countryside, with not a building anywhere in sight. I remember thinking that it would be very bleak indeed during the wintertime, which indeed proved to be the case. I suppose from the German point of view, it was an ideal place for a PoW camp being in an isolated part of the countryside. Suddenly, after a sharp bend in the road, we could see the outline of the guard towers reflected against the sky line.

As we got nearer we could see more clearly the guards in the towers watching our approach through their powerful field glasses. The barbed wire fences were now visible, and at last we reached the main gate which was opened to admit us into the camp. Scores of prisoners in various stages of undress were clustered all around in small groups to cheer and greet our arrival.

One of the many cartoons drawn by fellow PoW Bill Turner

    Once inside, we were given a pep talk by the Camp Commandant. The interpreter told us that the Commandant hoped that our enforced stay would be as pleasant as possible under the circumstances. What he really meant was that if we played fair with him, we need expect no unnecessary aggravation from him and his staff. He was on the wrong side of fifty, and I should imagine that he had seen service on either the Eastern or Western front. He had possibly been wounded, hence his posting to the comparative peace of a prison camp. He stressed the foolishness of attempting to escape as we would be faced with a hostile countryside, and even more hostile civilians.

    On the British side the most senior NCO assumed the role of Camp Leader and his role was to liaise with the German Authorities in the camp, and to look after the interests and welfare of the prisoners.

Stalag Luft 7 - Bankau

The Camp Leader pointed out to us the trip rail which ran around the whole of the perimeter fence, and was about thirty feet inside the fence. Under no circumstances were you allowed to step over the wire without the prior permission from the guard in the tower. Anybody doing so was liable to be shot, without any warning. If we were playing football or cricket, and the ball went over the wire, it was essential to attract the nearest guard's attention, and get his permission before retrieving it. Apparently there had been cases of PoWs in other camps absent-mindedly forgetting this all important rule, and as a result they were fired upon and killed.

Stalag Luft 7 was a new camp, and was still under construction. German and foreign workmen were still working on the main buildings, and the rumour was that it would be October time before they were habitable and we could move in. In the meantime we were allocated temporary accommodation on an adjoining site.

Our accommodation was primitive in the extreme, consisting of row after row of small huts which were made to hold about ten men - preferably of my size. Some wag had christened them 'coops', as they felt no bigger than hen coops! During the train journey to Bankau, I had got to know a tall thin pilot called Bill Turner who originated from the London area. We managed to keep together when we were allocated our billets. The huts were so low that Bill had to stoop to get inside, banging his head on the lintel if he forgot. We were issued with straw filled mattresses which we lay on the floor of the hut, and each prisoner was provided with a single blanket, tin mug and spoon.

The leader assured us that these were only temporary measures, and that once the main camp was completed we would be housed in proper barrack blocks, but for the time being we would have to grin and bear it. There were not any proper washing or toilet facilities either. A single hand water pump, situated near to the huts, served as the sole source of drinking and washing water for the whole camp. It must have been connected to a first class well, because it never dried up even with the regular arrival of new prisoners.

The toilet was even more primitive and was constructed in one corner of the compound. A huge trench had been excavated and enclosed by wooden screens. A long pole ran the whole length of the trench, and on which you perched when nature demanded, and in full view of everybody else doing the same thing. The whole of the pit was covered in a thick layer of lime, and a further supply of lime was stacked alongside ready for use as and when required. It was degrading to say the least, and was probably the cause of most of the complaints which the Camp Leader had to deal with.

The German Commandant was in overall command, of course, but the real power behind the throne was the German Security Officer. He was by far the most important man in the prison camp. It was his responsibility to make the camp escape proof, and to make periodic searches of the camp, and in particular the barrack blocks. To assist him in this work he had a staff of guards who not only manned the guard towers, but patrolled the camp continually.

Each of the guard towers were manned for twenty four hours by teams of guards and they were equipped with a machine gun and a very powerful searchlight. In addition each guard box was interlinked, and ultimately to the Guard room, by field telephone. The guards had powerful field glasses to keep us under strict surveillance at all times. There were also foot guards armed with rifles constantly patrolling inside and outside the wire, and guard dog handlers patrolled the camp once curfew had been called.

A special group of guards were available to carry out barrack room searches. Most of them could speak English so we had to watch what we said when they were seen to be prowling around. They wore overalls, as distinct from the ordinary guards who wore Luftwaffe uniforms, and they always carried long pointed sticks with which they constantly prodded the ground as they approached. These guards were aptly christened by the prisoners as "Ferrets", and the way they seemed to enjoy harassing the prisoners made them very unpopular.

A typical day in the life of a PoW would be to attend Roll Call at 7 am on the parade ground, under the supervision of the Camp Leader, until the arrival of the Commandant and his retinue. There were usually three German NCOs to do the ritual counting. Clutching paper and pencil, they would choose a row each, then would walk down the row tapping each of us on the shoulder in turn as they passed by, at the same time counting under their breath. On reaching the end of the column they would all confer and if any men had reported sick one of the NCOs would be dispatched to the coop to verify that he was in fact there. Then if all was well, and the numbers tallied their faces would light up and the senior NCO with a look of triumph would stride manfully up to the duty officer, give a smart salute and hand him the paper with the correct total, whereupon at this point in the proceedings we would let out an almighty cheer.

Unfortunately more often than not they would get it all wrong, and the whole pantomime would have to be repeated all over again. This was the signal for the lads to let forth with their cat calls, boos and groans. Of course most of us treated it as a huge joke and the fact was that we enjoyed taking the Mickey out of them. It was our way of getting back at them. Mind you it was a different story in the winter time, when the snow was on the ground and every one was frozen stiff and trying to keep as warm as possible. Some how it did not seem quite so funny then. I never did work out whether the Germans were as bad at counting as they seemed or whether they were so afraid of making a mistake that they were extra careful. The fact is, however, that anything over a hundred and they were in deep trouble.

Immediately after roll call in the morning there would be a dash to try to be first in the line for a wash. One of the major problems apart from the toilet - which was simply diabolical - was the solitary pump. The lads who had come on parade with towels round their necks, would immediately do a fifty yard sprint in an attempt to be first in the queue at the water pump and if you were not in that first batch you could forget it until later in the morning.

Bill and I found from experience that it was easier to go together and take turns to pump the handle while the other one washed. As for shaving, we would fill our mugs with water and take them back to the hut where we could shave at our leisure. Referring back to the toilet facilities we were constantly complaining via the Camp Leader, and the Germans were always going to do something about it, but of course never did. We had even suggested building a second latrine in the opposite corner of the compound and offered to supply the labour if the Germans provided the tools and materials, but they refused. Whether they were afraid of us trying to dig a tunnel, I don't know, but whatever their reasons for refusing, conditions got steadily worse as more and more prisoners arrived and we must have only ever been one step away from a serious epidemic of disease.

We would then disperse and go about our various chores. Each hut was issued with a broom and a pail which we were to use for drawing the water from the pump and so for convenience our hut decided to work in pairs to attend to the daily chores. We drew up a rota and each day two men would be orderlies for the day sweeping the hut out and generally tidying up. The water would be drawn from the pump and the daily rations drawn from the kitchen. The ration at that period was a loaf between ten men and the occasional issue of margarine and jam. Some of the lads tried to sub divide their slice in to three, so that they could have a little with each meal but their bread was wafer thin when they had finished trying to cut it. Most of us gobbled it all down at one go adopting the attitude of 'When it's gone it's gone!'. At lunch time the orderlies would collect the soup which was very thin, and reinforced with a few potatoes. It was not exactly top class cuisine and barely sufficient to keep us going but perhaps it was just as well we didn't know that we would have to learn to survive on a lot less.

After breakfast there would be the daily ritual walk around the perimeter fence, either singly or in pairs, passing the time of the day to one another as we met on the way round. We always had one eye on the ground looking for scraps of paper, wood, or anything that might be considered useful. There was a saying after the war that you could always tell an old PoW because he always walked around with his eyes permanently on the ground. I am not too sure about that, but I agree that life in a PoW camp brought out the instinct to hoard. Even today I am reluctant to dispense with anything, and the result is that I have a shed full of bits and pieces which might 'come in useful', but the trouble is I can never remember what I have saved, and even if I can remember - I can't find it!

What bit of grass there was had long since vanished on 'the circuit' as we called it, due to the hundreds of marching feet as they pounded the beat. It was the place where all the problems were solved and the world put to rights, and it did relieve the boredom. Every day was very much like any other day as far as we were concerned, and even the arrival of new prisoners caused excitement and would result in prisoners dashing over to the main gate to greet the new arrivals as they came in to the compound. The Camp Leader was a great believer in having a real and genuine welcome committee on hand every time there was a batch of new arrivals. He used to say that it was good for the morale of the newcomers to enter the prison camp to the sound of claps and cheers from the assembled prisoners around the main gate, but equally as important, it helped to demonstrate to the Germans our solidarity and determination not to allow events to get us down. Newcomers would be button holed for an update on the war, and occasionally prisoners would be reunited with former colleagues from their squadrons.

As the camp grew in size, we received sports and musical equipment, and books of all types, thanks to the Red Cross and other similar organisations. It was around this time that I managed to lay my hands on a prisoner's wartime diary and log book via the Red Cross.

Due to the efforts of such organisations, the camp was able to offer a wide range of scholastic and recreational activities to cater for most tastes. The prisoners shared their skills and talents by teaching others, especially foreign language classes. It never ceased to amaze me as to the wide range of talents held by many of the prisoners. Great interest was shown in music and the arts, and as more instruments became available more people were able to play their music even if they did not feel qualified to perform to the rest of the camp. But there were a number of professional musicians who could and did play for our benefit. We boasted a small orchestra who played the more serious types of music, and a small dance band who entertained us with popular tunes of the day.

Those of us who were not attending lectures could play football or cricket. We organised test matches between England and Australia, which caused much in the way of friendly rivalry between the two sides.

We were lucky that there was plenty of space for us to play team games here at Bankau, but it could prove a bit hazardous at times around the pump when drawing water. You had to keep one eye on the horizon for the odd cricket ball which might come whistling around your ears from out of nowhere.

As well as team games, there were other sporting events to be enjoyed. Two former professional boxers staged an exhibition bout one evening, and afterwards offered to coach any interested parties. Jimmy Ray and Jock were overwhelmed by the number of enthusiastic amateurs willing to learn the noble art of self defence, and boxing quickly became one of the most popular sports at Bankau. On September 4th we held a sports and athletics meeting, with races around the perimeter track, and I surprised myself by taking third place in the 100 yards sprint final.

The football committee had asked for interested prisoners to forward their names if they wished to take part in trials that were due to take place shortly in order to select the teams to represent the various nationalities that made up the prison population. Having played for the Post Office team in Wolverhampton, I submitted my name for consideration in my favourite position of outside left. Being a natural left footed player and reasonably fast, this was the position that I used to play back home.

Several trial matches were held, and I was lucky enough to be selected against Scotland in the first home international. The match was played on September 18 and watched by a good crowd which included some of the guards. Although the English team were trailing for most of the game, in the dying moments of the match, I managed to cross the ball and in a goal mouth melée, somebody

No Bacon and Eggs Tonight

forced the ball over line giving us a draw which we hardly deserved. One of the problems was the lack of proper strips, which meant we looked an ill assorted bunch when we were playing. But we never let that interfere with our efforts, even if most of us played in flying boots and ordinary shirts. Because of our physical condition, play was limited to thirty minutes each way, which believe me, was long enough.

Whereas I was more interested in sport, Bill was much more at home with a book. In fact, although we had become good mates since arriving at Bankau, we had very little in common really except our taste in music. Bill was an excellent artist and cartoonist, and he contributed many cartoons and sketches in my diary, for which I am most grateful. His talent for drawing did not go unnoticed, and there was always somebody coming in to pose for a head and shoulders portrait, in exchange for a few cigarettes or chocolate.

Whilst most of us were trying hard to make the best use of our time, there were some prisoners who became increasingly withdrawn and to all intents and purposes had given up the ghost. One morning, I heard a great commotion coming from a hut a bit further up the line and to my amazement saw a man being manhandled towards the pump by four burly prisoners. For a moment I thought it was a form of practical joke, but soon realised they were in deadly earnest. He was stripped naked and held under the pump, and scrubbed from head to toe.

By now a crowd had congregated around the poor wretch, and despite his protestations, the scrubbing went on until his skin positively glowed in the morning sunlight. Only then was he released and allowed to pick up his clothes and return to the hut.

Apparently he had taken to lying in bed all day and had refused to wash. He had been warned by his hut mates what would happen if he continued in this way, but their threats had no effect. In desperation they had complained to the Camp Leader, who ordered him to be publicly scrubbed. Some people might think it was rough justice, but cleanliness amongst ourselves under these primitive conditions was of prime importance. If any disease were to break out it would have spread like wild fire. Shortly after this unfortunate incident the Camp Leader issued instructions that all prisoners had to shave their heads and other parts as an extra precaution against possible disease. The barbers on the camp did a great job on us and we finished up like plucked chickens.

At long last, came the announcement that all of us had been waiting and praying for. There was to be an issue of Red Cross parcels and volunteers were required to distribute them around the camp. Red Cross food parcels were of American, British and Canadian origin, but all contained basic items such as tea, coffee, powdered milk, margarine, 'Spam', corned beef, dried fruit, cigarettes and chocolate. The British parcels usually had 'Nestles' powdered milk, whereas the American equivalent was 'Klim' (milk spelt backwards!). Either were most acceptable.

To everyone's intense disappointment, the amount was far less than we had hoped for, and only worked out at two parcels between ten men. There was no way that two parcels could be fairly divided into ten, so we decided to pool our resources and form a communal 'mess'.

Shortly after the arrival of the Red Cross parcels, we were instructed to remain on parade one morning instead of being dismissed. Suddenly, the main gates opened and the security officer leading his troop of ferrets suitably attired in their overalls and pointed sticks, marched into the compound. They entered each hut in turn, but concentrated their time on the huts housing the old lags, who had been in the camp since its opening. We thought that they must be looking for a radio, because rumour had it that one existed somewhere on the camp, and we were all worried should the search succeed in finding one.

Eventually we were allowed to return to the coops which were in a shambles. All our possessions had been pulled apart, and even worse our solitary tin of powered milk had been punctured by a sharp instrument. Gradually it became clear that the focus of attention was not a radio, but Red Cross parcels. Most of us had little to loose anyway but the old hands had quite a stockpile of tins. Some of it was found and the tins punctured, but much of their hoards were hidden elsewhere, well out of the reach of our zealous Security Officer and his bunch of performing ferrets.

The Commandant insisted that any future issue of parcels would have the tins punctured before distribution took place. The German High Command were well aware that food parcels had been used to feed escaping prisoners, and so they were determined to stop prisoners from stockpiling food. This was true of course in the large camps with good track records for organising escapes where prisoners contemplating escape were often given items of food such as dried fruit, chocolate and other such items, which could easily be carried by anybody on the run. This hardly applied to our camp, where we were not geared up to escapes on such a scale, and which did not have a store room full of Red Cross parcels.

Meanwhile, the work was proceeding according to plan on the new camp and when we had nothing better to do, we would stand by the wire and watch the workmen 'doing their stuff'. It was clear that we would be moving over very shortly, and it could not come soon enough for me. The toilet facilities were growing worse by the day and it was surprising that no one had fallen ill as a result. Also, the nights were getting distinctly chilly and we were having difficulty in keeping warm in the coops.

The Germans asked for volunteers to start cleaning up the new camp, so Bill and I put our names forward. With all the work going on in the new camp there was always the chance of finding the odd tool or other materials lying around. We managed to collect plenty of odd lengths of wood which the carpenters left lying around and which would come in useful for fuel. When the guard was called away, I managed to crawl under one of the barracks of the new camp and bury it in the relatively soft sand. We also found a length of twine, and I was also able to hide that safely and well clear of the eagle eyed ferrets.

We moved into the new camp on October 13th. The guards led us in batches of twenty out of the old camp and into our new barrack rooms where we were allocated a bunk. The buildings seemed to be well constructed consisting mainly of brick and wood. They accommodated about forty men, but they were long enough to erect additional bunks should the need arise. Two tier bunks had been erected with the usual wooden slats going across the bunk forming a base for the straw mattress. Wooden tables and benches had been provided, and in the centre of the room was a stove with a stack pipe leading out of the roof. In fact it was of a similar design to most RAF camps back home. Bill and I tossed for choice of bunks, and Bill won, choosing the top berth.

The biggest advantage gained from the move, was the greatly improved toilet facilities. The advent of flush toilets, and the added privacy that went with them, was beyond all belief. I remember strolling round the circuit one day on my daily constitutional, looking across to the old camp and in particular the primitive lime pit and pole, and wondering how we had managed to put up with it for all those months. Not everything in the new camp was perfect however. Unfortunately only one of the taps could be relied upon to work efficiently. This was ironic when you think that the old and much criticised water pump in the old camp never once let us down.

One day we were surprised when an unfamiliar PoW entered the barracks. He proceeded to tell us that from now on, we would receive a daily BBC news bulletin. He stressed the need for absolute secrecy and top security. We had always suspected that there was a radio hidden somewhere, and this development confirmed that. By necessity, the news was a much abbreviated version, but the basic facts were all there and we knew that it was all true. This made a welcome change to all the propaganda and lies which the Germans pinned up on the notice boards.

As the weeks unfolded, we evolved an elaborate system of signalling and surveillance, and had soon built up a very efficient security service throughout the whole camp. It soon became a proud boast that we knew the whereabouts of all the guards and ferrets the minute they entered the compound, and until they left again. The hiding place of the radio was known to only a few, but it was generally believed to have been smuggled in by the old lags when they first came to Bankau, probably stripped down into components and later reassembled.

On November 3rd, the long awaited stage equipment arrived out of the blue. The Commandant had agreed to let us use the largest building on the camp as a theatre, and once more volunteers were requested to assist in the erection. Bill and I volunteered again in the hope that the builders might get careless and leave some tools lying around. Because of my experience as a telephone engineer, I was asked to lay the electrical cables to the various lighting and power points ready for the electricians to connect their equipment. This entailed working under the floor, but being small this caused me no great problems.

It was whilst I was crawling on my stomach dragging a cable behind me, that I noticed three large sacks that had been

No Bacon and Eggs Tonight

discarded and conveniently left under the floor. Never one to look a gift horse in the mouth, I earmarked them for early removal back to the barracks. I had no idea at this stage what we could use them for, so I asked Bill for any suggestions. After giving it some careful thought, he came up with the brilliant idea of making them into capes ready for winter time. We were going to need something extra when the real cold weather arrived, and Bill's idea seemed a winner. We emptied them of the remains of the cement which they had originally held and hid them under our mattresses together with some electric flex that I had also helped myself to.

During our work on the theatre project, we had to borrow tools from the Germans which were kept in a large cupboard securely locked with a large padlock. Bill had noticed amongst the tools a very heavy duty knife, and he confided in me that he intended to borrow it permanently.

On the last day of our work on the project, we took the tools we needed under the eagle eye of the guard. Fortunately he was not in the habit of locking the cupboard until night time when all the tools were returned. Bill waited patiently for a chance to help himself. At last his moment came when the guard left the theatre and went outside. In a flash Bill pounced and scooped the knife up, and hid it down his flying boot. Later on I crawled under the stage once more and buried it in a safe place in the sandy soil. We held our breath when the tools were returned that night and the cupboard once more relocked. However, it looked as if we had got away with it.

A couple of days later I once more crawled under the stage and retrieved the knife and then carried it back to the barracks. With the aid of the knife, we undid the seams of the sacks, and cut them into the shape of capes, and refastened the seams with the twine that we had previously found. With the remnants we made hoods which went over our heads, and well down over the napes of our necks. Not exactly Saville Row tailoring, but nevertheless very effective. There was still enough left over to enable us to make two small rucksacks, fastened by lengths of twine. I have to admit that we looked a weird couple in our outfits, resembling two refugees from a monastery, and we came in for our fair share of rude remarks and laughter. However, we had the last laugh when those cold winter east winds blew across the parade ground whilst on roll call.

The capes were not our only effort at making good use of things that we found lying around. One day I was astonished to see one of the old hands boiling a tin of water on a queer looking contraption, and periodically turning a handle attached to it. He called it a "blower" and it was used primarily for making a quick cup of tea or coffee, using the minimum amount of fuel. It was designed on the same principle as a set of old fashioned bellows. The 'blower' had a crude fan constructed out of tin and wood from a bed board, and then fitted inside an empty 'Klim' tin. On turning the attached handle the fan would rotate inside the cylinder and a jet of air would be forced down a narrow tunnel, again made out of surplus tins, and leading to a shallow box in which you placed a small amount of fuel which might be grass, paper or rags. When ignited and the handle turned the air would cause the smouldering material to burst into flame. Bill and I were so impressed, that we constructed one ourselves, and it proved to be invaluable.

The Blower

One day, Bill had gone for his customary evening wash, when he noticed a claw hammer on the floor under one of the wash bowls. Thinking it might be a plant he was reluctant to pick it up, but the temptation proved too much in the end and he came bouncing back with it tucked under his battle dress tunic. It had obviously been left there by one of the plumbers, who were still working on the poor water pressure. The mystery is how it went unnoticed, as dozens of men, including myself had been in and out of the wash room all day, and yet we all missed it except Bill.

We were rapidly earning the title of the two best scroungers in the barracks, and it certainly proved the point that it paid to be vigilant at all times with one eye firmly on the ground. Fearing the possible backlash over the theft of the knife, and now the hammer, we decided that it would be more prudent to find a new and more secure hiding place than under the mattress. There was a space of approximately twenty inches under the barrack room floor, sufficient for a small person such as myself to crawl. We wrapped the tools and flex in odd bits of sacking and I decided that after roll call the following morning, I would bury them in the sandy soil. We asked the members of the barracks to keep a sharp lookout, and once I knew the coast was clear of nosy guards, I crawled under and buried the loot, marking the spot with a brick.

We were still waiting for the balloon to go up at any minute, but amazingly nothing ever happened. I can only assume that the guard had not noticed the disappearance of the knife, or being more concerned of the possible consequences to himself should he report its loss, had somehow managed to cover up the theft. Perhaps the plumber kept quiet for the same reasons.

Now that the theatre project was finished, the members of the Drama Group were now free to start rehearsals in earnest for the shows that were already in the pipe line. The first show to be presented at the newly named "Little Theatre", was a revue called "Compound Capers", and as the name suggests, was based on life as a PoW behind bars. It was intended to portray the funnier side of life as a prisoner of war. Strange as it may seem, life was not all gloom and doom, and from time to time amusing incidents did occur to some of us, and when they did we made the most of it. The script writers spared no one, and every amusing incident, no matter how embarrassing, was somehow woven into the show. Even the ferrets and the guards came in for their share of good natured fun, but they did stop short at the Commandant and the Security Officer, who up to now had not displayed any sense of humour.

I have always believed that satire in British comedy could well have been born and developed in a PoW Camp. Certainly, British PoWs had this ability to be able to laugh at themselves and their adversities, and were never afraid of taking the Mickey out of themselves; something which the Germans could not do, or even begin to understand. I am sure that on occasions the Germans must have thought we were completely mad. Courtesy invitations were sent out to the Germans, but the majority of those English speaking Germans who attended remained tight lipped, and did not appear to understand the British sense of humour. However, the show went down well with the bulk of the prisoners themselves, who apparently enjoyed the topical gags and sketches, and were generous in their applause.

The Little Theatre was always in great demand, and a day never passed without some function or other taking place. Bingo was a firm favourite with many of the men, but there was equally a lot of support for debates and lectures. Speakers were invited to talk to us on their own particular pet subject. These weekly talks were known as 'Fireside Talks', although the fire was conspicuous by its absence!

As well as the various types of entertainment on offer in the theatre, many prisoners continued to pass the time in studying. Unfortunately, now that winter was almost upon us, it was no longer possible to hold lectures outside. This caused a problem, and resulted in certain barrack blocks being used as classrooms, and the students tending to monopolise the tables and benches of some barracks. This did not go down too well with certain occupants. Tempers flared, and on occasions blows would be struck, and the rest of us would have to intervene before things really got out of hand. The winter weather meant that we found ourselves cooped up for longer periods, so I suppose it was inevitable that the problems which had been simmering away all the time suddenly boiled over. I am not suggesting that we spent the winter months picking fights with one another, but tempers did seem to fray more easily when you were struggling to keep warm, and cope with the ever worsening food shortages.

All this may seem very trivial, but in a camp of over one thousand men, and growing all the time, there were many different needs and personalities to be taken into consideration. Not everyone wanted to take part in sporting activities, and not everybody wanted to be 'Brain of Britain' either. Most prisoners were grateful to be alive, and many just wanted to see the war out and get home in one piece without any hassle. I am afraid that they regarded the invasion of the barrack blocks by the scholars as an intrusion of their privacy. There were precious few places where you could go to be private apart from your bunk, and to find your enforced home occupied by men learning foreign languages or working out mathematical problems was just too much for some of them to bear.

Eventually the Camp Leader worked out a compromise where a time table for different barracks was drawn up. This limited the use of any one barracks to one two hour session in any one day, and no more than three days a week. It was far from a perfect solution as everybody agreed, and many prisoners were still none too happy, but at least everyone had their say.

Considering all things, I suppose it was not surprising really that a few of the prisoners could not cope, and became intolerant of their fellow prisoners. It was surprising that there were not more who became "Stalag happy", which was an unkind way of saying that someone was having difficulty in coming to terms with the harsh realities of prison behind barbed wire.

All PoWs suffered from 'highs' and 'lows' throughout captivity, and the information we gained via our daily news bulletins was an influential factor on the mood of the prisoners. I can remember vividly the effect the news of the defeat at Arnhem had on all of us. The German propaganda machine was waiting for an Allied reverse, and they exploited it to the full. They filled their notice boards with vivid accounts of a great German victory, all in English of course, for our benefit. This plunged us into the depths of despair, and this feeling of despondency lasted for many days.

We had been delighted when we first heard of the drop at Arnhem, and the other bridges, and like most people the thought of failure never entered our heads. After all, since the D day landings we had become accustomed to success, so this reverse was hard to take. The more optimistic amongst us had been talking in terms of the war being over by Christmas, but alas, it was not to be.

The 17th November brought us much better news, and could certainly be counted as one of our 'high' days. The German battle ship The Tirpitz had finally been sunk. The Tirpitz had been a thorn in our flesh since the early days of the war, and had been responsible for the sinking of thousands of tons of Allied shipping. The Germans made no reference to this event on their notice boards. It sounded like the type of operation that 617 Squadron had been particularly trained for, and tailor made for the new Tall Boy or even its big brother Grand Slam, assuming that it had been delivered to the squadron. After the war I found out that 617 Squadron did in fact turn her upside down as she lay at anchor in a Norwegian fjord.

December 8th was another exciting day, when a cinema projector was delivered to the camp, probably thanks to the Red Cross, together with a film for our entertainment. Nobody seemed sure whether it was a gift or a loan, but what mattered was that the Commandant had given permission for them to show the film "Corsican Brothers" that night in the theatre. So many flocked to see the film, that the theatre bulged at the seams, and there were as many standing as sitting. The Camp Leader had to ask for permission to show the film twice a day for the rest of the week.

There was even better news to follow, for the following week another film was shown called "Andy Hardy" and featured a teenage prodigy by the name of Mickey Rooney!

I suppose that we must count ourselves extremely lucky in receiving a projector and films, theatre and stage equipment, and of course the musical instruments that had arrived at Bankau, taking into account the critical state of the German transport system. The Germans obviously would not give any priority to that sort of merchandise, and I can only imagine that they must have been in transit for a very long time, and that it was pure coincidence that they all seemed to arrive more or less together. However, I am certain that each and every one of us would have sacrificed the films, theatre and musical instruments in exchange for a regular supply of food parcels and warm clothing.

The first snow had fallen in early November, and since then we had moderate snow storms on and off, but on 17th December a blizzard raged over Bankau. However, even this was not allowed to interfere with roll call and parade, and we had to attend as usual. The roll calls were taking longer each day, and the guards were making heavy weather of the head counting. Even allowing for the fact that the prison population had trebled since my arrival, the situation was deplorable. As a result, the men became increasingly bitter and ready to explode.

Another cause of bitterness at this time was due to the fact that the ferrets appeared to be stepping up their searches. They would select a barracks, possibly because they suspected something was afoot, or just for the pure hell of it, and order everyone outside, irrespective of the weather whilst they conducted their search. They would go through everyone's belongings, strip the beds and mattresses, and anything else that happened to be lying around before calling it off and leaving us to clear up the mess. On the rare occasion that they did find anything that they could confiscate, they would hold up their booty like overgrown school boys, so that everybody could see how clever they had been.

It was not surprising that the ferrets were detested by all PoWs in all of the camps throughout Germany. Strangely enough, we could stomach the ordinary guards, but not the ferrets and their sneaky ways.

Guards throughout prison camps were referred to as 'goons'. I have no idea where the name originated from. A national pastime enjoyed by PoWs was that of 'goon baiting'. This took many forms, and the object was to lose no opportunity to 'get one over' the guards, rather in the same way that the ferrets tried to harass us at every turn. It was largely carried out in a light hearted manner, and the aim of the exercise was to remind the Germans that our spirit and resolve was as strong as ever.

The guards quite often wandered into the barracks and very often around brew time, whether by luck or design I'm not sure, but sometimes the lads would invite them to a drink of tea or coffee. Thanks to Red Cross parcels and personal parcels sent from home, many prisoners had built up extensive stocks of tea and coffee, as well as cigarettes and chocolates which were far superior to the rubbish issued by the Germans.

Usually the guards were only too happy to accept the offer, being aware that it would be superior to what they had available. Most of them understood a limited amount of English, so if somebody was in the mood for a bit of goon baiting, he would probably shout across the room "How do you like a proper cup of coffee, Fritz? Better than the rubbish Hitler gives you?" Then after a bit more banter somebody else might say, "I am going to report you to the Commandant for drinking with the prisoners, and you will be sent back east to see the Ruskies again!" Most of the guards knew we were only baiting them, and just carried on drinking their tea smiling to themselves, and generally taking not the slightest notice of the mild insults. But if it happened to be a new guard who had not experienced it all before, then the very mention of the Eastern front and the Russians was enough to make them pale before your eyes and dash out of the room, leaving their drink unfinished, amidst howls of laughter from the lads. Most of the guards had been on the Eastern front at some time or another, and had only been sent back because of wounds or illness, and I am quite sure that they would sooner be dead than be sent back to endure the terrible conditions

At Bankau, our baiting was quite mild, but in the big camps like Sagan and Thorn, they had developed goon baiting into a fine art. Certain guards would be earmarked, and bribed with flattery and items such as cigarettes and chocolate. Once the guards had been compromised in this way it was easy to blackmail them. Guards had been known to smuggle cameras, film, radio parts, and even German documents and passes into the camps. All essential items for any prisoner thinking of escape from a prison camp. Here at Bankau, we had not developed to that stage because we did not have the resources such as cigarettes and chocolate to bribe the guards with, and at this stage of the war it was unlikely that we ever would be in that position.

However, this did not stop the almost weekly rumours flying around about the imminent issue of food parcels. It did raise morale for a few hours but the anti climax on realising that it was yet another rumour was quite devastating. I saw many men just break down and cry on learning that it was just another cruel hoax.

However, shortly before Christmas, the Camp Leader announced that there really was a truck at Bankau railway siding containing Red Cross parcels. We suddenly had visions of parcels every week right up until Christmas, and we thought our fortunes were changing for the better. First the theatre equipment, projector and films, and now the one thing we craved above all else - food parcels! Once again everyone's spirits took an upwards turn, and it was no wonder that there was a host of prisoners volunteering to unload the wagon.

Unfortunately, when the guard unlocked the wagon it was immediately clear that there were nowhere near the number of parcels as shown on the invoice. Of course it was impossible to trace the missing parcels. We had learned from our own experience of German rail travel how unreliable it was at the present time. The wagon had been in transit for weeks, and could have been held up anywhere during that time, lying dormant in some sidings and at the mercy of all and sundry. I have no doubt that the railway workers and troops had been helping themselves to Red Cross parcels now that the food crisis was growing, even though they faced severe penalties - even execution - for looting.

However, all this was speculation, and the hard facts remained that there were not as many parcels as there should be. Once again, we were going to be bitterly disappointed, and it was with a mixture of sadness and anger that the remaining parcels were loaded onto the cart and brought back to the camp. There were sadly only enough parcels for one issue, and it was decided under the circumstances to hold back the distribution until the 23rd December, which seemed to be the only sensible thing to do. Prior to distribution, the ferrets had a field day puncturing all the tins.

We had found from experience back in the old camp that it was more economical and easy to 'mess' in groups of ten, and we had continued with that arrangement since moving in to the new camp. One of the men in our group who rather fancied himself as a culinary expert volunteered to provide us with a Christmas dinner. He announced to the rest of the group that he was going to make a bread pudding for us, and that he would need the whole of one day's bread ration, biscuits from the food parcel, as well as most of the dried fruit. Seeing the look of concern on our faces, he hastened to assure us that he knew what he was doing and having no wish to offend him, we agreed.

No Bacon and Eggs Tonight

On Christmas Eve, he crumbled all the bread and the plain biscuits together in a tin bowl, together with margarine and the dried fruit. He had previously prepared some milk from the tins of powdered milk, and added that to the weird looking mixture. I have to say that at this stage it looked a revolting mess, but nobody wanted to say anything.

At lunch time on Christmas morning, he went over to the kitchen to collect the cooked pud. By this time the orderlies had returned with the soup and potatoes which we ate as our first course. At last the big moment came, and with a look of triumph on his face he served each of the group a portion and then covered it with more of the milk. I have to say that it certainly tasted better than it looked in its raw state, and was quite the tastiest thing any of us had eaten since becoming PoWs.

We all thoroughly enjoyed it, and came in for some envious looks from other groups. After the meal we washed up and then settled down for the rare treat of a cigarette. We proposed a vote of thanks to the chef for providing us with a good meal, then some settled down with a book, whilst others played cards, much as we might have done had we been spending Christmas at home. The only thing that was missing was the Christmas tree - and the Christmas drink - but there was nothing we could do about that.

"Cooking"

It was much later in the evening when we had the first sign that all was not well. One or two men complained of violent stomach pains, followed later by more of us. The British Medical Officer came over to see what all the fuss was about, examined us, and then asked us what we had been eating or drinking. When we told him about the bread pudding he was horrified, and tried to explain to us that our stomachs had contracted due to the near starvation diet we were receiving from the Germans, and the worst possible thing we could have done was to indulge in overloading our stomachs with sudden amounts of stodgy food. He gave us medicine to take, but warned us that it might take two or three days before we finally got it out of our systems.

Due to the strict curfew, we were sealed inside the barracks after the nightly head count, and so a bucket at the end of the barracks served as a toilet. However, if the bucket was insufficient for your needs, you had to hammer on the door and attract one of the patrolling guards who would release you and escort you to the toilet block. Needless to say, 'the bread pudding bug' meant that we had to have a guard posted permanently all night long outside the door. The guard insisted that the door remain locked, which was ridiculous considering the state we were in. The only escape we had in mind was escaping to the toilet.

On Boxing Day morning, no one from our group was fit enough to go on parade, and after a while one of the guards poked his head round the door and came in to count us as we lay in our bunks, feeling like nothing on earth. When the men were finally dismissed, we received no sympathy from them at all. Apparently the guards were running around like maniacs trying to locate ten missing men, which meant all prisoners had been forced to remain on parade until it was sorted out. We heard later that the guards thought there had been a mass escape. Apparently nobody had bothered to inform the Germans that ten men had reported sick. No wonder we were not too popular at that moment in time with the rest of the prisoners.

I am afraid that our chef took it all very badly, feeling that he was to blame for all of the problems by making the bread pudding, and even although we told him that we did not hold him responsible in any way, he announced that he wished to stand down from his self appointed role of chef, and hand over the duties to somebody else.

The next event on the calendar was the advent of New Year's Eve, and we left the organisation of the festivities in the capable hands of the Scottish contingent. We had received permission from the Commandant to use the theatre, and to extend the curfew time to allow us to see the New Year in. We were treated to Scottish music and songs played by the accordion band, and even an exhibition of Scottish dancing on the stage. The talents of the prisoners knew no bounds. The entire audience appeared to be enjoying themselves, joining in with the singing. No doubt most of us were hoping that, God willing, this would be the last New Year any of us would be spending behind barbed wire. There was a strong rumour that the Russians were ready to launch their final all out offensive of the Eastern front. The Germans were being compressed ever tighter on all sides, and that was the best possible news as far as we were concerned.

Perhaps as we sat there singing and celebrating the arrival of the New Year, it was just as well that we were not to know of the hardships that lay ahead of us in the very near future. At the stroke of twelve, we started to sing 'Auld Lang Syne', and wished each other a happy new year, and a speedy end to the war. Unfortunately we had nothing stronger than tea, coffee or water to toast each other with, but that did not seem to matter.

On January 2nd, we paraded as usual for roll call, and once again the guards made a hash of the count. They had several recounts without success, and the mood of the frozen prisoners on parade became distinctly ugly. Feelings of bitterness and resentment had been building up for many weeks, and in a belligerent mood, some of the more militant broke ranks and legged it as fast as they could to the comparative warmth of the billets. I winced, expecting the guards to open fire, but mercifully they

Stalag Luft 7 - Bankau

refrained from doing so. Some of the guards were sent to round them up at gun point, which caused even greater delays, and eventually they were returned to the parade.

Unfortunately the matter did not rest there and the furious Commandant subjected us to two extra parades morning and afternoon for the next three days as punishment.

Life as a PoW brings out the best and the worst in people. It was about this time that allegations were made that two prisoners who had been working in the kitchens had been holding back part of the food ration for their own consumption.

Investigations of the charges were made, but reached no satisfactory conclusion either way. Personally, I always mistrusted these alleged accusations, which I believed were as a result of jealousy, but either way, the two men had lost the confidence of their comrades. As a result, the Camp Leader wisely decided that the two men should be replaced.

As a result of these allegations and the 'breaking ranks' episode with its resultant extra parades, morale was low. Anti-German feeling was running very high, so it was felt that the Commandant and his retinue should be invited to the opening night on January 8th of a new revue, "Pantomania", in an attempt to 'build some bridges'.

The decision was by no means unanimous, but it was felt that the Germans may have considered it vindictive had we not asked them, and that it might have rebounded on us in the long run. The Commandant accepted the invitation, probably for similar reasons as we had asked him. At any rate everyone's honour appeared to be satisfied.

They duly arrived before curtain up, but it was noticeable that the Security Officer was not amongst the party. The interpreter sat next to the Commandant throughout the performance, and was kept busy for the benefit of the German party. They appeared to enjoy the show - at any rate they laughed in the right places even if they were later than everyone else. It was a good show, with the squeaky falsetto voices of those characters in 'drag' causing great amusement.

The following day, excitement rose when the magic words "Mail up!" were heard in the barrack room. On hearing these words, everyone would stop what they were doing and the whole place would become as silent as the grave. Anxious faces would light up when they heard the sound of their name, and they would depart to their bunks clutching their precious envelope like a child on Christmas morning. The fact that the letter had already been scrutinised by the censor did not seem to matter. It was difficult for the unlucky ones not to show their disappointment and to put on a brace face, inwardly hoping that next time around it would be their turn. I was one of the lucky ones, receiving a letter from my mother, my first since the end of November. Her letter was restricted in its contents due to the censor's pen, but she was able to tell me that she had received a letter from me, and was relieved to know that I was safe and well. We were restricted, if I remember correctly, to writing two letters and two cards per month, but there was no limit to the amount of incoming mail you could receive. But there was no guarantee that you would receive them in the right order!

A letter was a great morale booster, and the receiver would walk around on cloud nine for many hours after the event. Prisoners worried about their families back home in just the same way that relatives worried about the welfare of the prisoners. Knowing that all was well back home was a big load off a prisoner's mind, making imprisonment easier to bear.

Unfortunately not all the letters were the bearers of good news. One could sympathise with prisoners who received news of the death of a close relative or friend, but it was far more difficult to know what to say to a colleague who had been informed that their wife or fiancée had left them for somebody else. I feel that if some of these wives or girlfriends could have seen the anguished looks on their faces, they might have acted differently, or at least postponed telling them until they were in a better environment and mental state to deal with it.

The weather by now was bitterly cold, and for most of us if was our first experience of the arctic like weather that prevailed in Eastern Europe at this time of year. The fuel supply was getting worse, and the already small coke ration had almost stopped. We were forced to rely more and more on daily trips to the nearby forest area to collect wood for the kitchen and stoves. Prisoners would carry out this task with the aid of hand carts, under the supervision of a guard. Even with the wood ration we could not light the stove for long each day.

We would spend most of the day and night wrapped up in every stitch of clothing we owned, and in exceptionally cold weather would take to our beds with the blankets pulled around our ears. Bill and I always wore our capes and hoods in bed when the temperature was at its lowest. The worst affected areas were extremities, namely hands and feet. We wore old socks as gloves, but our feet suffered worst, and even with warm flying boots, my feet were permanently cold. It truly was a miserable time for all of us.

Going for a strip down wash required a great deal of will power in these freezing conditions, and it was easy to see that one's personal hygiene could suffer if you did not grit your teeth and make the effort. We were still living in hope that some parcels might get through from home containing warm clothing, and we always stressed the need for it in letters home, but if we were honest most of us realised that it would be unlikely at this stage in the war.

Rumours were rife around the camp that the Russians were making good progress, having started their long awaited winter offensive, and the news of the progress of the American and British armies on the Western front was most encouraging. We speculated what would happen when they reached Bankau, which could not be far off now. Would we be left in the camp to await the arrival, or would we be moved to a place of safety as laid down in the Geneva Convention? We were in a tricky situation, and it would be silly to pretend that it did not cause us concern.

We also noticed an uneasiness amongst the guards. They seemed to be losing their cockiness, and those of them that could speak a little English were much more ready to talk to us about the outcome of the war, and some of the better English speakers would even discuss the situation at great length. This would have been unthinkable even a few months ago. They were scared of being overrun by the Russian armies, and were still hoping that the American forces would reach Bankau first. The Germans feared Russian reprisals as a result of the terrible atrocities both sides had committed against each other.

By now we could be in no doubt that the gun fire coming from the east was getting much closer. At night we could look out of the barrack room windows and witness the Russian star shells as they burst and illuminated the skies. It was like watching a gigantic fire work display on November 5th, but of course the implications were much more sinister.

As a result of a meeting held by the Camp Leader, we set about our preparations for a possible evacuation in earnest and took stock of everything we possessed. We had little or no food, but we did have a small amount of tea, coffee, and dried milk which we had managed to hide from the ferrets during their frequent searches. We took just enough for our immediate needs, and the remainder was shared out. Some groups had nothing in reserve and would have to rely completely on German rations when the time came to move. Bill and the rest of the group watched out while I crawled under the floor and retrieved our trophies. I knew the exact spot because I had marked it with a brick. I retrieved them quickly and smoothed the soil over before returning to the safety of the barracks with the booty. We were taking a chance of course, hoping that if there were any searches in the near future the Security Officer would not pick

Stalag Luft 7 - Bankau

on our block, but as it happened the ferrets seemed to have more important things on their minds.

Bill and I decided to take the blower along with us, but this meant that we would need a supply of fuel. We sacrificed two of the bed boards, and with the aid of the knife, split them into very small pieces. We also scrounged around for any odd scraps of paper. We packed the tools and all our fuel into the two rucksacks, and used a piece of flex to make harnesses for them to go over our shoulders and necks, saving another piece of flex ready to tie the blower onto the rucksacks. We were ready to move if needs be.

17

THE FORCED MARCH

We were summoned to parade as usual on the 17th January by the call of Jack Stead and his bugle. There was nothing at this time to suggest that it was going to be any different today from any other day. Roll call was held as usual, and for once they seemed to get it right first time around, but instead of dismissing the parade, the Commandant called the British Officers and Camp Leader over, and entered into a lengthy discussion with the aid of an interpreter. The Camp Leader returned to the assembled parade and called us to order.

He announced that he had just been informed that due to hostilities developing on the Eastern front, the German High Command had decided in the interests of safety to evacuate Bankau immediately and we must make ourselves ready to leave. We were to reassemble in one hour's time ready to move off straight away. No transport was available except for a horse drawn cart for the sick and wounded. Each prisoner would receive two days marching rations, and arrangements had been made for a horse drawn field kitchen to go ahead to the first scheduled stopping place where we would all receive a hot meal after the day's march. Everybody would need to take some form of drinking utensil with them, and it was in our own interests to keep the luggage down to a minimum. He strongly advised us to wear all our available clothing, as we would be exposed to severe winter conditions for long stretches of time.

The Forced March

He added that he had pressed the Commandant as to our ultimate destination, but had received no direct answer, neither would the Commandant give him any assurance as to what type of accommodation would be available on route. The reason there was no transport available was as a direct result of the indiscriminate bombing attacks being waged against the German people.

With these grim words ringing in our ears, the Camp Leader dismissed the parade, and we all trooped back to the barracks for the last time to complete our packing. We had been expecting it for the last week, and it was more a question of when rather than why. The gun fire over the last week had been getting much closer, and it was clear that the Germans would have to make the decision to evacuate, or await the arrival of the Russians. Nevertheless, now the day had finally dawned, most of us were very anxious to say the least, and the gloomy talk of the lack of transport did nothing to reassure us.

Back in the billet, Bill and I draped our blankets over our shoulders, and secured them with twine, and then we donned our home made capes and hoods, making sure that the hoods were pulled well down over the napes of our necks. I looked around the room at the state of our colleagues as they went about their final preparations and realised how totally ill equipped we all were to undertake such a march under arctic conditions and on a near starvation diet. Bill and I were better off than most, with our capes and hoods which had already proved their worth during the long hours on the parade ground during roll call. But most of the lads were clad only in battle dress and flying boots, plus roll necked pullovers. Some did have flying suits, and one or two had their leather jackets, but this was the only protection they had. Most of the men tried to make crude forms of head gear resembling turbans out of odds and ends. Some were lucky enough to have their forage caps which could be adjusted to allow the flaps to come down over the ears and give protection against the icy east winds. Most of us had managed to scrounge old socks which we wore on our hands to act as gloves. In addition I had my good pair of flying boots with leather soles and stout fleecy lined tops.

No Bacon and Eggs Tonight

I made what was to be my last entry in my diary to the effect that we were preparing to leave Bankau for a destination unknown. I then stored it away in my rucksack, and there it stayed for the remainder of my confinement in Europe. I fully intended to keep it up to date, but I was soon to find that through sheer fatigue, hunger and cold I was incapable of making the effort. All my energies would be used in a battle of survival. We decided to take it in turns to carry the blower, and Bill volunteered for the first spell. Fortunately, it was not heavy, although a bit bulky. I fastened it onto his haversack, and we had a final look around before sitting down to await the call to go on parade.

As it happened, the start was postponed until 3.30 a.m. on January 19th. Jack Stead summoned us once again, and we left the billets which had been our home for a long time, complete with our pathetic bundles which included our blankets. I heaved a sigh of relief that it was not snowing.

One by one the prisoners trooped out of the barracks and started to form up in two rows outside. Some of the prisoners had spent the last few days building sledges with timber taken from bed boards, the theatre and other buildings. They had fastened ropes made from the flex from light fittings onto them, so they could be pulled by teams of prisoners. The musicians, reluctant to leave their precious instruments to the tender mercy of the Russians, appeared with them strapped to their backs. We must have looked an ill assorted bunch to the observer, but then this was not going to be a fashion parade. We were each provided with our marching rations, and the Camp Leader and the Padres took their place at the head of the column. The horse driven cart holding the sick and wounded left the compound, and proceeded on its way. The Medical Officer, taking as many drugs as possible, left with the sick accompanied by guards. Everything seemed ready, and at a given signal the long column of prisoners started to move off slowly. Guards fell in either side of the column as we got under way. I am sure that everyone at that moment in time must have felt concern as to the eventual outcome of this mass exodus.

The Forced March

The last of the column left the gates of the camp, which had once echoed to the sound of hundreds of voices and now stood silent as the grave, and we proceeded in a westerly direction as we started on our journey to the unknown, illuminated by the searchlights. At last the guard towers were no longer visible and we had taken our last view of Bankau Camp forever.

My account of the march is a little sketchy as I am relying from memory plus notes from fellow PoWs, and reports made by the Camp Leaders and the Red Cross after the cease fire was implemented. In some cases I have not been able to check the accuracy of the names of the places we passed through owing to border changes between Germany and Poland after the war, and resultant changes in place names. The Camp Leaders' report states that the Germans had said that for every man who fell out of the column on the march, five men would be shot, but I have no recollection of whether this had been officially announced or not.

It is difficult to see how the Germans would have known if anyone was missing, as we were not subjected to any count before we left, and so they could not have been certain how many prisoners were marching. It would have been simple enough for some of the more militant prisoners to take a chance and hide themselves in the now empty camp.

Our first overnight stop was Winterfeld, about thirty kilometres from Bankau. I cannot remember our accommodation, but it may have been a barn. I vaguely remember making a brew of tea on the blower using melted snow. I recollect it tasting odd, but at least it was hot. We left at 5 a.m. and arrived at Karlsruhe five hours later, where we were accommodated in a brick factory. An additional field kitchen had been provided as the original one just could not cope with fifteen hundred men. This shortened the queues for the soup, although the amount and quality was no improvement on the night before. We managed to make another brew of tea on the blower. The brick works at least afforded good shelter from the arctic like conditions, which was what we needed above anything else. We lay huddled together in small groups, trying to keep each other warm, but sleep was difficult even though we were dog tired and ached in every limb due to the cold and fatigue.

We left Karlsruhe the same night and marched, in temperatures as low as minus 13 degrees Centigrade, to Schonfeld. The Medical Officer, and the two Padres did a tremendous job at this stage in pleading with the stragglers and back markers to keep going. Many just wanted to be left alone on the road side, saying that they had reached the end of their tether and could go no further, but to do that would have proved fatal. Nobody could have survived in those exposed bitterly cold conditions for long. It must have taken a lot of persuasion and bullying to keep those lads moving.

We arrived at Schonfeld at 9 a.m. where we were issued with biscuits and coffee before settling down to rest in various cow sheds and barns. The British Medical Officer declared several men unfit to march due to sickness and frostbite. The British Officers dug their heels in and refused to allow the men to march until the Germans provided additional transport for the sick. Eventually after much argument, the Germans relented, and managed to obtain another horse and cart from somewhere for the latest cases of sick men.

I suppose this could be considered a minor triumph for the British Officers in squeezing this concession from out of the Germans, but in reality there was little else the Germans could do, unless they were going to leave the prisoners behind and leave them to their own resources. I suppose that some poor farmer was told to provide the Germans with transport whether he liked it or not.

By 5 a.m. on January 22nd we were under way again. The Camp Leaders' report states that some men were slow to leave due to being unable to find their baggage, and the Germans entered their quarters and 'discharged their firearms'. The same report says that at this point 23 men were missing, and it is unclear what had happened to them.

The Forced March

The guards resumed their positions on either side of the column, but by now the column was so stretched that the guards were very thinly spaced. When we halted briefly for rests we were able to slip into the fields and dig up potatoes and sugar beet from under the snow. The guards saw what we were doing of course, but made no attempt to stop us. Most of them were well beyond the first flush of youth, and quite honestly, I think they had reached the stage where they could not care less what happened to us, and like us just wanted to get the war ended.

The guards' rations were not all that good either, consisting of bread and sausage, which they used to munch as they marched alongside us. I don't know if they got a hot meal at night, but somehow I don't think it would be much better than ours. On the other hand they did have transport on which they could rest when they had completed their stint of marching. They seemed to march for two hours then rest for two.

Most of the time we prisoners stumbled forward blindly, with our heads bowed to shield us from the driving snow and fierce winds, following in the wake of the man immediately in front, and totally unaware of what was going on around us. We stopped when the man in front stopped, bumping into each other. When the column stopped for a ten minute rest we would collapse onto the road side.

The marching was beginning to take its toll. One by one the sledges were abandoned, as the prisoners became too tired to pull them, and even the musicians started to discard their instruments. Some exchanged them with villagers for bread, but chiefly they were just abandoned on the roadside. It must have broken their hearts to do such a thing, but it was taking us all our time to carry ourselves. The blower which Bill and I were carrying was fortunately very light.

I think that most of us had thought that they would have found transport for us after the first few days, but it was obvious that it was going to be foot slogging all the way. It would not have been so bad if we had been aware of our ultimate destination, but despite all the protests, the Germans remained as evasive as ever on the subject. I began to wonder whether they were deliberately taking this course hoping that starvation and exhaustion would take its toll, and partly solve the problem that we presented them with. It was clear that they could not care less about us, and they would probably have welcomed us to make a mass escape if it was only to give them the excuse to shoot us.

Bill and I were determined to keep up with the main body of marchers, and so far we had managed to do that reasonably well. Although Bill and I spoke little whilst marching in order to conserve our energy, a firm bond had formed between us, and through it we were able to help one another when we were going through a particularly bad patch.

My boots were standing up well, and my feet seemed to keep fairly warm whilst we walked, but the minute we stopped and the blood stopped circulating, they quickly reverted to ice bergs. Our capes and hoods had done us proud, and as a result we had managed to keep our blankets reasonably dry from the frequent snow storms. But the less fit and poorly clothed were suffering enormously, and were falling further and further back, and the entire column was becoming very stretched indeed. At this stage the biggest problem was frostbite, but there was little the doctor could do for that. Many prisoners after spending time on the carts, were finding that even though they were still suffering, they were having to make way for more serious cases. This was the pitiful state we had been reduced to, where the Medical Officer was having to make the heart rending choice of who amongst the sick were most capable of walking again.

The column eventually reached a place called Jenkwitz, which was to be our next stopping place. I cannot remember what our accommodation was, but I vaguely remember being herded in to barns. Again, the officers and leader tried to find out from the

The Forced March

Germans our ultimate destination, but they would not or could not give a satisfactory reply. Repeated appeals for transport fell on deaf ears.

On reaching our next stopping place, Wansen, the Medical Officer was so alarmed with the condition of most of us, that he demanded a complete halt for twenty four hours in order that we might regain some of our strength. The cases of sickness, frostbite and dysentery were growing by the day. The Medical Officer had only been able to bring whatever drugs he could carry, and by now could give the precious medication to only the most serious cases. The Germans reluctantly agreed, but the rest period ended only too soon, and by 4 a.m. on the 25th January we were on the road again. Apparently, we rested at two more villages, Heidersdorf and Pfaffendorf, although I have no recollection of this. One day's march was very like the previous. By now we were all stumbling along like drunken robots hardly noticing where we were.

We arrived at Standorf on the 28th January, where the Medical Officer called for a complete halt due to the worsening condition of some prisoners. We left at 6 p.m. on the following day, staggering on in darkness under blizzard conditions to the small town of Peterwitz, and it was clear even to the Germans that we had reached the end of the line. The British Officers made it clear to the German authorities that they could no longer be held responsible for the welfare of the prisoners, and unless something was done regarding the provision of transport then they would be faced with many deaths, which Germany would be held accountable for. We were then allowed to rest up for two days, in an attempt to revive our aching bodies and minds.

So far the distance marched was an incredible 210 kilometres, without seemingly getting anywhere. Our route had started off in a westerly direction, and then south until we crossed the River Oder, and then westwards once more, before finally turning north. It appeared that this U-shaped route had been designed to keep us clear of Breslau which was a prime target for the Russians.

On February 1st, we left once again and struggled as far as Prausnitz, where once again we rested. The Medical Officer was adamant that we could walk no further, and requested a full scale meeting between our leaders and the Germans. The outcome was that they would arrange transport by rail from the town of Goldberg, and we were to remain here until the necessary arrangements were completed. This was the best news we had heard since leaving Bankau back on January 17th. It was while we rested at Prausnitz that our supply of coffee and tea finally ran out. It had not been possible to make a brew every night after the days marching, and sometimes we were too exhausted to even attempt it. Nevertheless the supply had lasted well, and although the drinks were made with melted snow, they had helped. We laid the faithful blower to rest at Prausnitz.

Fortified by the news of our impending transport, we left on the 5th February for the remaining miles to Goldberg where we were to board the train. When we left Bankau, we never thought that we would have to walk so far, and I believe that far from making concessions, the Germans had already planned to march us to Goldberg. That would account for their steadfast refusal to discuss our destination. We finally arrived at Goldberg in a deplorable state, but our ordeal was far from over as we were soon to find out.

We shuffled into the railway sidings at Goldberg, not knowing what to expect, but lined up on the railway track were rows of cattle trucks. We were herded into these trucks as though we were animals. Most of us were so weak, that we could not get aboard unaided, and the stronger ones had to assist the sick and weaker ones. The guard was counting us in, and when he had a full quota he slid the doors shut and then secured them with a huge bolt, thus effectively sealing us in. The whole process must have taken well over an hour.

The Forced March

There were between fifty and sixty men in the truck, and it was obvious that we could not all sit down with our backs to the wall. Our first consideration was to the sick, and we settled them down against one of the end walls, and made them as comfortable as possible. Other prisoners sat down against the walls, and the remainder sat in the centre, supporting one another back to back. We quickly worked out a rota, whereby we all took our turn sitting against the wall.

The conditions in that truck defy description. We were all filthy, and stunk to high heaven, which was not surprising considering that none of us had been able to wash since leaving Bankau, but added to that, some of the sick were suffering with dysentery. The stench was unbearable, and was not made any easier because there was only one grille about eighteen inches square set into one of the walls to provide any ventilation at all, and this was totally inadequate for the number of men in the truck. It seemed that we had escaped from one horror only to find ourselves in an even greater one. As often happens in moments of crisis, someone took charge and assumed command, urging us to do something about our predicament.

The first important task was to arrange some form of toilet facility especially for those with dysentery and other stomach problems. Somebody reported that they could see a chink of light, and on closer inspection we found that there was a hole of about two inches in the floor where one of the boards had slightly rotted. The leader asked if any of us had any tools, and Bill and I produced the knife and hammer. Another man had a small iron bar which he had found in the brick works early on in the march. All of us had been tempted to discard these items to lighten our load, but fortunately our combined instincts for hoarding and our tenacity, had now paid off handsomely.

We set to work with the tools, and managed to prise the rotten portion away, but cutting the adjacent boards was not so easy. Eventually, using the knife as a chisel, we were able to cut a deep groove across the boards, and then with the bar we managed to wrench out the boards leaving a hole in the floor approximately twelve inches square. This was ideal for the lads with dysentery and other stomach disorders, as they could now squat down over the hole when necessary. Meanwhile, the train had at last pulled out of the siding, on what we all hoped would be the last lap of our journey, although we did not know our destination.

We next turned our attention to the grille, to see if it could be enlarged to give us more air, but it was too well reinforced, and we had to abandon the idea. The walls of the truck were made of planks, about eight inches wide, nailed to vertical struts spaced about four feet apart. On inspection, it seemed as if sections of the planking had been renewed at some time, probably due to rot. There seemed to be one four foot length which had recently been renewed, so we decided to concentrate on that section. The work was hard, and we were in no fit state for manual graft of this nature. Nevertheless, we set about it with enthusiasm, working in shifts, in an effort to lever the plank away from the uprights. The iron bar was invaluable, and I doubt if we could have managed without it, because they were thick planks and secured with long nails. After much effort we managed to prise it sufficiently to enable us to get the bar in the crack, and then lever it out a little more. Using the knife, we attempted to cut the fixing nails one by one and eventually they broke in two.

At last one side was free, and by rocking the plank backwards and forwards, we were able to loosen the other enough to insert the bar and wrench it clear. The plank fell onto the floor of the wagon, and we were immediately rewarded by a draught of fresh air from the gap in the wall. Our success was worth all the hard work, and we gulped the fresh air in greedily.

Conditions were much better in the truck now, and if any of us felt in urgent need of fresh air, we could get up and breathe in the pure air through the gap in the wall. The train frequently stopped, and sometimes we would be shunted in the sidings for hours on end,

The Forced March

but they never once opened up the truck to allow us to alight to attend to nature. We were quite well off in our truck, because we had constructed our hole in the floor, but I shuddered to think how they were faring in other trucks.

It was daylight on the following morning when we found ourselves being shunted into yet another siding. We immediately banged and shouted as loud as possible, demanding to be let out. Eventually the guard came and we heard him slide the bolt back, and open the huge door. One by one we staggered out, assisting those who needed help. Afterwards the guards appeared with large jugs of water and each of us was allowed one cup full of the precious liquid. We had been inside that truck for twelve hours, and it was our first chance to set foot outside. Only too soon, we were ordered back inside at gun point, and we took up our positions once more according to the rota. We were destined to endure this nightmare of a journey for three days, and during that period the trucks were only opened twice a day; late evening before dark, and again at first light. After the initial stop where we received water, the policy seemed to be to shunt us into a siding for the night, wherever possible, thus leaving the track clear for what they would consider more important traffic.

Before we left Prausnitz we had been issued with a ration of bread and margarine, also a minute portion of some non descriptive meat, and some of us had a few raw potatoes and sugar beet left, which we had confiscated from the fields during our stops on the march. Our rations were then shared out with those less fortunate than ourselves. However, all our food had gone by the second day, and apart from that one cup of water, we received no food or drink from our captors for the whole of that period on the train.

On the fourth morning we started to roll early, and it was not too long before we pulled in to yet another siding. Somebody looked out from our home-made window, and informed us that we had arrived at a place called Luckenwalde. He could see the name on the sign quite clearly from his vantage point. We wondered whether this place was going to be journey's end, or if it was just another casual stop. Whatever the reason for stopping, it was clear they were going to have to give us food and water soon or they were going to have corpses on their hands. Our condition had deteriorated still further, and some of the lads who had dysentery were very dehydrated, and we were desperately worried about their condition. They needed expert medical attention straight away. We remained in the sidings without anyone opening up the doors. At long last the guards appeared, and to our joy commenced to open up the trucks. We were ordered to alight and bring all our possessions with us. This was journey's end.

We staggered out of the truck, as before, and lined up. But the guards did not bother to count us, and we left the sidings walking at a snail's pace. Even though we barely had the strength to lift our paltry bundles, we somehow managed to carry the desperately sick men. Eventually the familiar sight of barbed wire, and guard towers came into view. As the head of the column neared the camp, the outer and inner gates were opened to allow us to shuffle inside. It probably seems a strange thing to say, but at that moment, I am sure that all of us were glad to be behind barbed wire again. At least we were with friends, and would have time to try and recuperate and rest.

We had emerged from a nightmare which had lasted twenty one days, and in that time we had shuffled along for 240 kilometres on a near starvation diet, and in terrible weather. In addition we had endured three days shut up on that train, sixty men to each cattle wagon, with no toilet facilities. We received no food on the train. But most terrible of all, for thirty six hours we received no water. One can possibly excuse the lack of food, because the guards and civilians were suffering almost as badly, but there was no justification in denying us water to drink. There were no water shortages in Germany, and the long halts in sidings offered plenty of opportunity to open up the wagons and allow us to drink. It seemed to us that they had deliberately embarked on this policy in the hope

The Forced March

that there would be widespread deaths, and which would have been one way of solving the problem which we presented to them.

They would have been able to claim that in the spirit of the Geneva Convention they had moved us to safety away from the battle zone, but in doing so had treated us as less than animals and reduced us to a state from which it would be months before we recovered physically. There were many times when we expected some of our colleagues in the cattle trucks to die. Some prisoners of course may well have been scarred mentally for ever more. The Germans had a lot to answer for and we all held them in the greatest contempt and hatred.

The distance marched by us would have been exceptional going for fit soldiers on top rations and with first class equipment, but to have been achieved by us was almost unbelievable. I am sure that it was only the unflinching spirit and desire to live that kept us going in the face of such intense cold and hunger. The rations per man for the twenty one days was three loaves of bread, twenty four rye biscuits, and a modicum of meat, which was used mainly in the soup, and a small amount of margarine and jam.

We were not the only column of prisoners on the road of course. During this period of the war, a staggering 76000 prisoners of war of all nationalities were being forced marched over varying distances from camps all over Germany.

If indeed the German plan was to cause as many deaths as possible throughout the march, then they totally underestimated the determination and will to survive of all the PoWs who took part in that march in 1945, but it would be too much to hope that they all survived and lived to finally see the end of the war and return home.

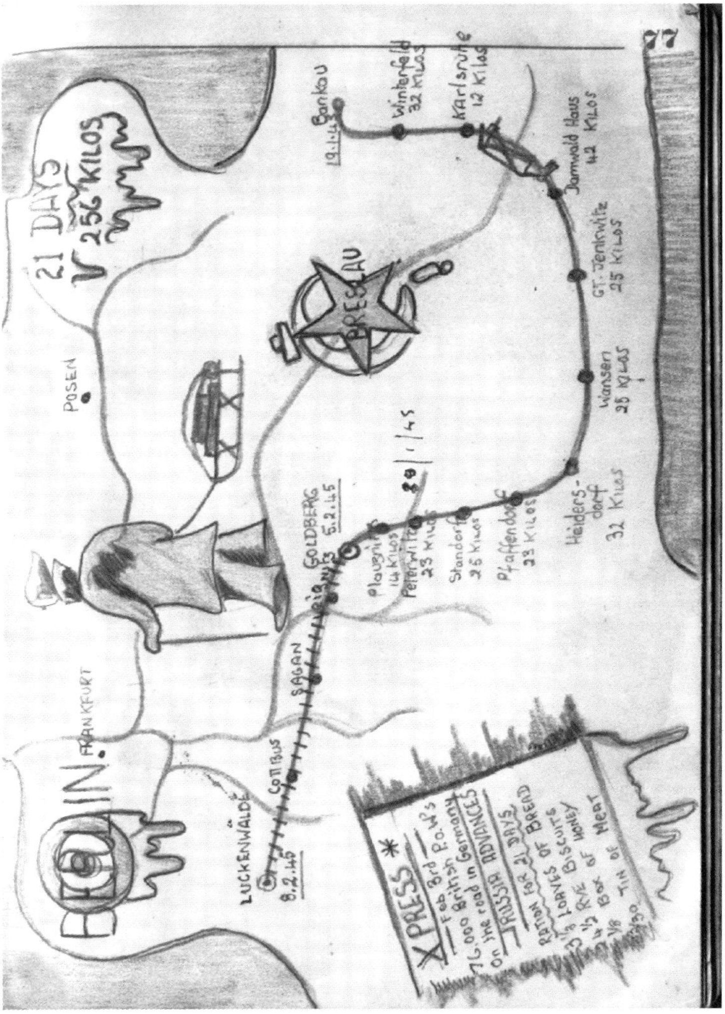

21 DAYS
256 KILOS
FRANKFURT
POSEN
LUCKENWALDE
8.2.45
COTTBUS
SAGAN
GOLDBERG
5.2.45
Peterwitz
23 Kilos
Standorf
25 Kilos
Pfaffendorf
23 Kilos
Heidersdorf
32 Kilos
Wansen
25 Kilos
GT. Jenkwitz
25 Kilos
Jarnwald Haus
42 Kilos
Karlsruhe
12 Kilos
Winterfeld
32 Kilos
Bankau
19.1.45
30/1/45
XPRESS
Feb 3rd P.o.W's
76,000 British in Germany
on the road in
RUSSIA ADVANCES
RATION FOR 21 DAYS
LOAVES OF BREAD
RYE BISCUITS
BOX OF HONEY
TIN OF MEAT
77

18

STALAG 111a LUCKENWALDE

There was no shortage of helping hands when we entered the camp. The Senior Medical Officer at Luckenwalde was there, together with our own, and they quickly arranged for the worst cases to be admitted to the hospital, with every chance that with the right treatment they would eventually make a good recovery. In the meantime the rest of us were separated in to batches, and put through the delousing centre before being allocated accommodation. We were offered changes of underwear, which were badly needed by us all, and were then given a good portion of hot soup, which helped to revive our aching bodies. It was quite a while after arriving at Bankau, that we learned that many of the resident prisoners had voluntarily relinquished their daily German ration of food in order that we new arrivals might have extra rations for the first few days, in an effort to start the rebuilding processes so desperately needed by our bodies and minds. Undoubtedly, we were at a very low ebb both physically and mentally when we first entered Luckenwalde's gates. The healing process would not happen over night, and it would be many months before we would be able to resume a near normal existence as prisoners of war. The generosity of our fellow prisoners knew no bounds, and was just another example of the comradeship that existed between all ranks and nationalities behind barbed wire.

By necessity we were separated into small groups and dispersed amongst the already crowded barrack rooms. Bill and I managed to keep together and we were allocated to a particular barracks. They were equipped with three tier bunks, but most of them were already occupied. Most of the newcomers, including Bill and myself, had to be content with sleeping in the passage way between the bunks. It was not comfortable of course to our emaciated bodies, but we were not complaining. At least we were reasonably safe and dry, and above all out of the cold winter winds. The biggest problem was that if anybody needed to get up during the night it was almost impossible not to walk on the men sleeping in the passage way. Quite often you would be woken up during the night to howls of protest as somebody's foot landed on somebody's face or some other part of the anatomy!

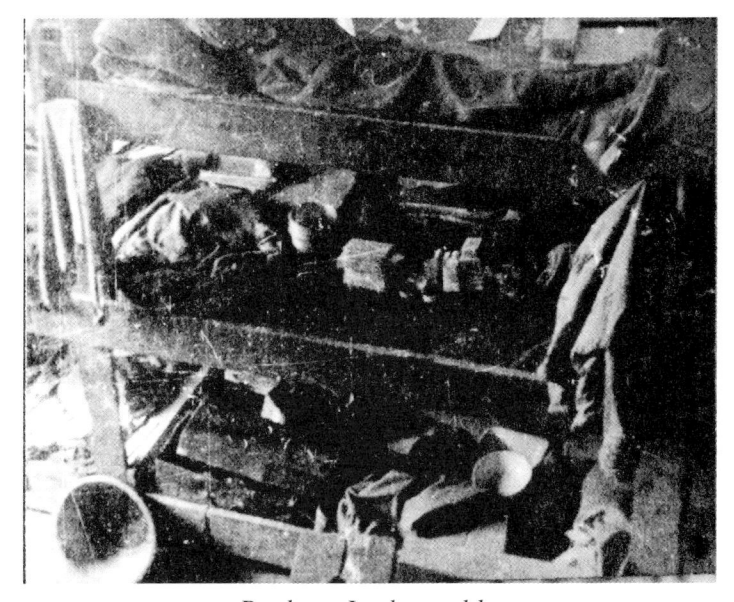

Bunks at Luckenwalde

Gradually as the weeks rolled by, our morale which had reached rock bottom during the march began to improve. We started to take much more interest in what was gong on about us, and this was a good sign, but our physical condition still gave cause for concern. We simply were not getting sufficient of the right type of food to enable us to put on weight. It was perhaps just as well that

Stalag 111a ~ Luckenwalde

there were no full length mirrors to see ourselves. I remembered looking at Bill, and thinking he resembled a walking skeleton. I have no doubt that he held similar views about my appearance.

As we slowly began to regain our strength, Bill and I resumed our walks around the perimeter track. It resembled Blackpool promenade on a busy Saturday, except there were no candy floss stalls, or side shows. Nevertheless, scores of prisoners trudged their way round and round, often on their own, with collars turned up braving the snow and wind. Apart from the exercise, it was the only place where you could gain any privacy to ponder on things. Often I would wait until the perimeter was relatively free from walkers, and then I would embark on two or three circuits on my own. There were precious few places where you could go if you felt in need of solitude. Even the toilets had been stripped of their doors, probably in the endless search for fuel.

Picture obtained at Lukenwalde, origin unknown

No Bacon and Eggs Tonight

Luckenwalde was a large camp in comparison to Bankau, but it was already bursting at the seams long before our arrival. It was one of the camps that had been selected as a reception camp for 'marchers' like ourselves from other camps, and as a result there were three times as many men held there than the camp was designed for. It was a multinational camp, and there were separate compounds for the British, American, French and Polish prisoners. You were not supposed to be able to move from out of your specific compound, but in reality it was relatively easy to do so, and the prisoners used to roam around pretty much as they liked. It was almost impossible for the guards to keep track of so many men. This freedom of movement was quite different from Bankau of course, where we were always under the scrutiny of the guards. The Germans still held roll calls and made the outward show of counting heads, but we got the impression that they didn't really have a clue as to how many men were held in the camp. I suppose, they were ready to throw in the sponge, and leave us all to it. Undoubtedly we had become a major nuisance to the German authorities, and this did not fill us with any confidence as to their future behaviour and our welfare.

Picture obtained at Lukenwalde, origin unknown

Picture obtained at Lukenwalde, origin unknown

Picture obtained at Lukenwalde, origin unknown

One thing that did not seem to have been affected as a result of the influx of all the extra men was the flourishing black market. The long term PoWs with Red Cross parcels, cigarettes and other items to spare, spent their days wandering from compound to compound trading and doing deals. I am afraid that us 'marchers' could do nothing but stand by and watch the more affluent conduct their deals.

There was one major exception to this freedom of movement and that was the Russian prisoners. They were housed in a separate compound, and segregated from everyone else. It was the one compound that we could not enter. We sometimes caught glimpses of them as we walked around the perimeter fence, but that was all. I suspect that the reason for separating them from everyone else was because the Germans did not wish us to see the pitiful state of them. Neither side believed in observing the Geneva Convention with one another, and it was common knowledge that the Russian prisoners were treated worse than animals and were on worse rations than us. Both sides were committing terrible atrocities on one another, with executions and deaths as a result of their harsh treatment. I have no doubt that the German prisoners in Russia were being treated in much the same way, and I shudder to think how many PoWs on either side died or were shot whilst in captivity.

Sporting activities appeared to be at a minimum. Small groups of prisoners could be seen kicking a football about haphazardly, but with no great enthusiasm. Mind you, with all the additional prisoners that had arrived, there was very little room to carry out organised sport, and all of us who had been on the march had neither the energy or inclination to take part. I never thought that I would see the day when I would not wish to take part in a game of football. I am inclined to believe that there was a general feeling of apathy beginning to creep in now that the end of the war was in sight, and the older prisoners were unconsciously just 'marking time'.

Stalag 111a ~ Luckenwalde

Picture obtained at Lukenwalde, origin unknown

Quite often the American 8th Bomber fleet would fly overhead at great heights either going or returning from a bombing mission. On these occasions, having nothing better to do, we would all troop outside and peer into the sky following their route. We used to follow the condensation trails that the Liberators and Fortresses made from their huge four engines as they ploughed through the air. The planes themselves only looked like flies, and were very difficult to see with the naked eye. They seemed to meet with very little opposition from German fighters, probably because the American fighters were now providing escort. However, the German anti-aircraft fire was still something to be feared, as I had good reason to remember. One day we were watching the bombers flying in a westerly direction homeward bound after a raid somewhere in Germany, when we suddenly saw one of the bombers become detached from the tight formation and begin to lose height rapidly. It was too high to see whether it had been attacked by fighters or not, but I suspect that flak was the cause. We spotted six or seven parachutes open, and followed their progress down as long as we could, but they eventually dropped beyond our horizon, and we lost sight of them. They would probably have landed a long way from the camp, and we could only hope that they were safe and well and did not land in the war zone.

We still received our daily news bulletin from the BBC, and it was clear from the tone of them that things were continuing to go well for us and that the German forces were being compressed into an ever tighter circle. Both the Allied and Russian armies were making steady progress, and I do not think that any of us really thought that there could be any major set back now. Prisoners were even talking again about being home for summer, and some of the more enterprising prisoners were opening 'books' and taking bets on the actual date of the end of the hostilities. Quite a number of cigarettes were changing hands as a result.

The German rations were getting less as the entire structure of the German economy began to crumble even further. Their fuel supplies were now almost dried up, and they were finding it difficult to find petrol for their tanks and military vehicles. The effect of the decision by the American 8th Bomber Forces and our own Bomber Command to concentrate the bombing of their oil supplies and the rail network was paying dividends. Altogether it must have been causing tremendous problems to them as they tried to supply and reinforce the battle zones.

Food parcels were now a distant memory, except for those camps who had reserve stocks. There must have been thousands of parcels stored in warehouses throughout Germany, but we would never see them because the Germans were either unwilling or unable to deliver them. I wondered why, with all the cards stacked against them and defeat staring them in the face, the Germans did not sue for peace, if only to save further loss of life amongst the military and civilian population. Of course, we were not to know how fanatical Hitler and his followers really were, and how much hold he had over the German people and the military. Those who did criticise and plot against him were dealt with brutally. The men who were involved in the unsuccessful bomb plot against Hitler were put to death in the most barbaric fashion. They were suspended from hooks in the ceiling by piano wire around their necks. No quick and merciful death for them. This was the type of men that Hitler and his regime were like, utterly ruthless, and with no regard for human life.

With the domestic fuel supply almost non-existent, organised wood gathering parties went out daily, under escort, in order that we would have fuel at least for cooking in the kitchens. They would return with grisly stories as to the state of the civilian population as they struggled to stay alive. Our ration was growing less, and we wondered where it would all end and whether we would even survive until the end of hostilities. When we first arrived at Luckenwalde, the bread ration was one loaf between ten men per day, which was little enough. Now it had been reduced to one loaf between twelve, and there was talk of reducing it still further. Fortunately we were still receiving our daily soup ration but that depended on fuel. If that were to dry up for our kitchens, then we would be in real trouble. When distributed, the bread ration for each man was two thin slices per day, and believe me they were thin.

I was always hungry like everyone else, but I tried not to let it dominate my life. However, some of the lads had become so obsessed that they seemed unable to talk or think about anything else but food. They would lie in their bunks at night, telling all and sundry the mind boggling dishes they were going to order once the war was over. Naturally, this eventually proved too much for the rest of us and they would be told in no uncertain manner to belt up. Things would quieten down for a bit after these outbursts, but before long they would be back on the old subject and we would have to suffer whilst they rabbited on.

It was around this time that men complained about having their bread ration stolen. As I said, nobody got the chance to steal mine. Nevertheless, it was a most upsetting incident, and affected us all. Naturally suspicion fell on everybody, and we all went around feeling as if everyone's eyes were on you. The thefts continued, and one particular man was suspected of being the culprit, and it was decided to set a trap for him. He fell for it and was caught red handed. He was carted off in tears to go before the senior British Camp Leader. We never did discover his fate, but he was never seen on the compound again, which was just as well because a lot of men were gunning for him. He must have been desperate indeed to stoop so low as to steal his comrades' food. We were all hungry, but most of us managed to keep things under control, whereas he didn't. The culprit was actually the first man to complain about the thefts. Whether he thought that that would draw suspicion away from himself I don't know, but it didn't work and he paid the penalty.

The sound of gunfire from the east reminded us that the war was getting ever closer, as the Russians continued to make progress in their advance along the Eastern Front. We all lived in hope of the Americans arriving at Luckenwalde first and relieving the camp. In fact all the reports and news bulletins remarked on the speed of the American advance and suggested that they would soon be here. What we were not to know, of course, was that on nearing the River Elbe they slowed down drastically. It has been suggested that this was a deliberate move, politically motivated, to allow the Russians time to launch their all out final attack on Berlin itself. If this is correct, then the politicians were already sowing the seeds that were to lead to the Cold War of later years between the Soviet Union and the Western Alliance. We wondered what our fate would be when the time finally arrived for the Germans to evacuate Luckenwalde and prepare for their last stand in and around Berlin. Logic told us they would be forced to leave us as they could no longer guarantee our safety as there was nowhere else to take us. All those prisoners who had taken part in the march were neither physically or mentally equipped to undertake another mass exodus.

As the net tightened still further around the German armies, we received further bad news regarding our already miserable food ration. The rumour mongers were right, I regret to say, and our miserable rations were cut again. The bread ration was now one loaf between sixteen men, and the soup ration on which we depended

Stalag 111a ~ Luckenwalde

was now void of any meat at all, and even the amount of potatoes was reduced. This was a body blow to us all, and the effects of malnutrition were beginning to affect the health of many of the prisoners. The worst affected were the former marchers who had never really received sufficient food in order for them to make any marked progress. The Swiss and Swedish Red Cross were fully aware of the situation, their last visit to Luckenwalde being in February just after completion of the march. They promised to do whatever they could to relieve the situation, including the delivery and distribution of Red Cross parcels, but we all knew there was little they could do other than protest on our behalf. The German infrastructure was collapsing around our ears, and we could only hope and pray that the war ended before it became too late for any of us.

Day by day the gun fire became louder from the east, and at last we were forced to accept reluctantly that we were not going to be liberated by the Americans and we quietly set about making preparations for our meeting up with the Russians. We were very concerned about the eventual reactions of the guards and the German troops once they knew their last chance of saving the war had gone. Would they take it out on us, and start a shooting match here in the camp, with POWs as targets? We were in no doubt that they would be quite capable of committing atrocities against us as the cold blooded execution of fifty RAF Officers from Sagan prison camp was still fresh in our memories. Now that we were reputed to be under control of the civilian government and not the military, our position was even worse.

Briefings were held throughout all the compounds to discuss these all important issues, and whilst nobody wanted to exaggerate the problem, it was necessary to have some plan ready, should the shootings start. It was decided that in the event of any mass shootings, rather than lie down and accept the inevitable, we would try and rush them in the hopes that some of them could be overpowered and their weapons seized. It was around his time that a tragic event took place. Apparently the pressures and privations of life behind barbed wire had become too great for one prisoner. One day whilst walking round the circuit, he dashed over the trip wire, rushed the fence and attempted to climb it. His mates who were walking with him, were taken by surprise and were unable to restrain him. The guard from the watchtower opened fire on him, and he slumped back to the ground having been killed outright. Fortunately his mates showed great presence of mind, and resisted the temptation to go to his assistance, otherwise they would certainly have been killed as well.

He was buried locally, and fellow PoWs formed a guard of honour. It was doubly tragic to have happened at this stage of the war, with liberation just around the corner. Whether he had planned it or whether it was on impulse we shall never know, but obviously his mind must have been in a turmoil. The relationship between guards and prisoners from that moment on became even worse, and we let them know our contempt for them at every opportunity.

It was clear that the Russians were very close at hand. Once again we were witnessing the star shells at night as they illuminated the skies and the gun fire was increasing in its ferocity. It was a strange and frightening position to be in, with the Russians on one side and the Germans on the other. We should have been delighted at the prospects of liberation, and obviously there was great excitement mounting throughout the camp, but it was tempered with caution.

We knew by now what we might expect from the Germans, and we had made our plans to deal with that emergency should it arise, but the Russians were an unknown quantity as far as we were concerned. The guards were getting extremely jumpy by now, with very good reason. Before much longer they would be either dead or taken captive, and on their way to a Russian PoW camp in the depths of Siberia. Events were beginning to turn full circle. We were anticipating freedom, and they were facing life behind barbed wire.

Our worst fears appeared justified when a party of SS troops arrived in the camp accompanied by the Commandant and his staff. They appeared to be deep in conversation and went through a tour of inspection before leaving the compound. Later on, the Camp Leader announced that the Commandant had advised him that we were now under the direct control of the German Field Commander who was responsible for defending this sector of the war zone, and all future orders would originate from him. We were instructed to carry on as normal, and providing that we carried out all orders that might be given to ensure our safety, we would come to no harm. I am afraid that none of us were convinced by these words, and this was reinforced when we saw that SS troops had replaced the guards in the towers and on foot patrols.

I went to bed feeling anxious and wondering what the future held for us. The noise of the artillery was deafening and it was impossible to get much sleep. Most of us spent the night watching the free fireworks display from the windows but gradually the noise and star shells subsided and we retired to our bunks, and I must have drifted off into a disturbed sleep.

It was already dawn, when I woke to the shouts of "The guards have all gone!" Leaping out of our bunks, we crowded the windows, and scanned the landscape. We were astonished to see not a single guard anywhere. The guard towers were deserted and there were no signs of any foot guards. They seemed to have evaporated into thin air. It took a moment or two for the full impact to dawn on us, then we started to cheer and sing at the top of our voices. We forced the door open and trooped outside. By now other barrack rooms had joined us outside, and the compounds were full of laughing and cheering men, congratulating each other and shaking hands. We were like young children released from the classroom at playtime. It was quite some time before the cold morning brought us back to earth, and one by one we returned to the barracks, shivering, but feeling on cloud nine.

We were relieved that the SS had left without taking their revenge on us, and we were grateful that our worst fears had not materialised. The one topic of conversation was "How long will it be before the Russians arrive?" The Camp Leaders quickly arrived on the scene to confirm that the SS had left during the night to take up fresh defensive positions. For our own good we were told we should refrain from leaving the camp until the position became more stable. They stressed that we were not out of the woods yet, and although the Russian vanguard was not far away, the orders were to stay put in the interests of safety. These were sensible instructions of course, because there was bound to be fighting going on around the camp and obviously the leaders did not want any stray bullets coming our way.

These were tough words for us to swallow, considering that we had been waiting for this day to dawn for months, and for some prisoners, years. Some of the more militant were all for ignoring the orders and wanted to walk out to meet their liberators. However common-sense prevailed, and we waited patiently for our first sight of the Russian forces. The Camp Leaders were in a difficult situation now that the Germans had gone. They had to assume full responsibility for the safety and welfare of the prisoners in the camp, and yet they fully understood and sympathised with our desire to walk out of the gates if only for a few minutes as free men. None of us could really feel free until we were on the other side of the barbed wire for good. The leaders reminded us of the fact that the Allied Commander in Chief had issued a directive for all PoWs to remain in their camps until they had been relieved and officially repatriated by the Russian forces to the American Army Commanders, and that this would receive top priority.

19

FREEDOM (OR IS IT?)

By now, crowds of prisoners were standing around the compound gates to gain a good vantage point for when the Russians arrived. Others, safe in the knowledge that there was no one to fire on them from the guard towers or patrolling foot guards, crossed the trip wire and lined up around the wire fence. There was a sense of expectancy all around, and people were talking very quietly. It was barely two hours since the Camp Leader's announcement that they were on their way when a faint rumbling sound was heard in the distance. The noise got louder by the minute, and then suddenly out of the gloom appeared an armoured car, followed by two tanks and a lorry load of soldiers. The Russians had arrived at last. They stopped outside the gates which were already open, and they alighted from their vehicles grinning all over their faces.

It is hard to describe the scenes that followed over the next hour or so, except to say pandemonium reigned supreme. Months, and in many cases, years, of frustration and bitterness were suddenly released in a tide of emotion. Laughter, joy and tears were all in evidence, and people were falling over one another in an effort to shake the liberators by the hand. The Russians, obviously impressed by their reception responded likewise, with back slapping and handshakes all round. Complete strangers might have been forgiven for thinking that we were long lost friends, meeting again after years of separation. It seemed at this moment that all our fears about the Russians were unjustified, and some of us felt guilty for harbouring such opinions about them. Russian speaking prisoners from the

Polish compound acted as interpreters and before long a proper dialogue was established between us all.

Russian Soldiers at Luckenwalde

It appeared that the main body of troops had bypassed the camp and were in pursuit of the German forces who were retreating in the general direction of Berlin, where the final chapter of this long and bitter war was soon to be settled. Our liberators were part of a detachment which had been deployed to make contact with us and defend us against any possible reprisals or counter attacks by isolated groups of SS troops who were known to be fighting a rear guard action in the area. The Russian Military Command were well aware of the existence of Luckenwalde, and once the support troops arrived in the area, they too would be Berlin bound, but for the time being they were more than happy to make our acquaintance. They were a weird looking bunch, including Mongolians and women soldiers, but were all heavily armed with automatic weapons and rifles. Glad as I was to meet them at this time, I would not have liked to have fallen foul of them under different circumstances.

Freedom (or is it?)

By now the festivities were in full swing, with singing and dancing, and the exchanging of cigarettes. One of the Russians produced an accordion from somewhere and started to play Russian dance music, and soon feet were tapping in time with the rhythm of the music. Some of the Russians began to dance energetically to the music and very soon there were attempts by the PoWs to copy the Russian style of dancing, which caused great amusement amongst our liberators.

Eventually, more through exhaustion than anything else, the festivities died down and we prepared to move back to the barracks for a much needed rest, but not before witnessing the antics of the freed Russian prisoners. The fittest amongst them climbed aboard the vehicles, waving newly acquired rifles and shouting at the top of their voices "Hitler kaput", and "Berlin! Berlin!" and working themselves into a frenzy. I would not like to have been in the shoes of any German unlucky enough to come into contact with these hate filled fanatical Russians. I never found out what happened to the sick Russian prisoners who must have greatly outnumbered the fit ones, but the Russian compound that held them all in isolation from the rest of us, was now empty as if by magic. No doubt they would be well looked after from now on.

From time to time we heard isolated bursts of gun fire, so presumably the rear guard action by the German storm troopers was still taking place in the area, but as the day wore on the firing became less, and it really looked as if the war had at last passed us by. Our newly made friends told us not to venture out until they notified us that it was safe to do so, and the immediate area around the camp had been cleared of all Germans. Apparently, many German snipers were holed up in buildings, and still causing casualties among the Russians. With that they left the vicinity of the camp, and once more peace reigned over us all. The rest of the day was a bit of an anti climax after the excitement of the morning. We took advantage of our new found freedom by wandering freely throughout the length and breadth of the camp, discussing the events of the day with friends old and new.

I along with many more climbed the ladder to one of the guard towers to survey the scene both in and out of the camp. I was surprised that there was no activity going on outside and that there was no sign of any Russian troops. Even though the main body of fighting troops would have passed us by now in pursuit of the Germans, I thought there would have been some sign of the advanced unit which liberated the camp. I assumed that they would be somewhere in the vicinity, even if not visible. I went to bed that night feeling more secure than I had for months.

The following day we were informed by the leaders that the Russian support troops had now arrived in the area and had been in touch regarding the day to day running of the camp. They regretted that in the interests of our safety, we could not be allowed to wander out of the camp as and when we wished and that until final arrangements were completed regarding our repatriation we would have to remain inside the camp. Although the guard towers would not be manned and there would be no patrolling foot soldiers, the main gates would be locked.

After our initial disappointment at being locked up again inside the camp, there was some good news for us. Due to the food shortages certain prisoners were selected to accompany the Russians on food foraging excursions in the area. Requests were also made for men with experience of work in abattoirs and butchering, as well as cooking. At least the Russians were taking positive steps to feed us and involving us in the process. This was taken as a good sign. We all believed we would be repatriated very soon, probably within two weeks at the outside.

The next few days passed smoothly enough, despite being confined to camp, and there was a much more relaxed atmosphere now that the Germans had fled. Bill and I were still trying to come to terms with the turn of events and the novelty had not yet worn off. The foraging parties seemed to be having a certain amount of success, and arrived back at camp with carcasses of slaughtered animals on their carts ready for the butchers to do their work. The

Freedom (or is it?)

result of this was a huge improvement in the soup ration. For the first time, it was liberally laced with meat, which may have been of unknown origin but none the less very tasty. True, the bread ration remained the same, but it really looked as if things were beginning to turn the corner at last.

Someone from the British contingent had entered the German Administration block and was surprised to find that all of the prisoners documents relating to their captivity were carefully filed away in alphabetical order according to nationality. It was suggested that perhaps the prisoners would like to keep them as souvenirs of their enforced stay in Germany as non-paying guests.

In order to cope with the demand in an organised and efficient manner, they were distributed in barrack room order. Eventually our barrack was called, and Bill and I and all the other interested men took our place in the queue. I gave my name and service number, and one of the volunteer clerks went over to one of the huge filing cabinets and returned with a brown envelope containing my documents. So good was the filing system that the whole proceedings took less than a minute. The envelope contained the original forms and photographs that had been taken when I was at the Interrogation Centre at Frankfurt. It was my first chance, of course, to examine my documents closely. There was a brief description of me in one of the sections, my finger prints, and the two far from flattering photographs with the placard around my neck displaying my service number. There was even a small additional envelope containing the negatives stapled to the form. It seems ironic that the Germans could find transport to convey all these documents from Bankau to Luckenwalde but could not, or would not, find transport for desperately sick men during the forced march. They had also made it a priority to file them all again on arrival at Luckenwalde. Nobody could have accused the Germans of inefficiency in their administration set-up!

The days were slipping by and we were naturally becoming concerned over the lack of news relating to our repatriation. When

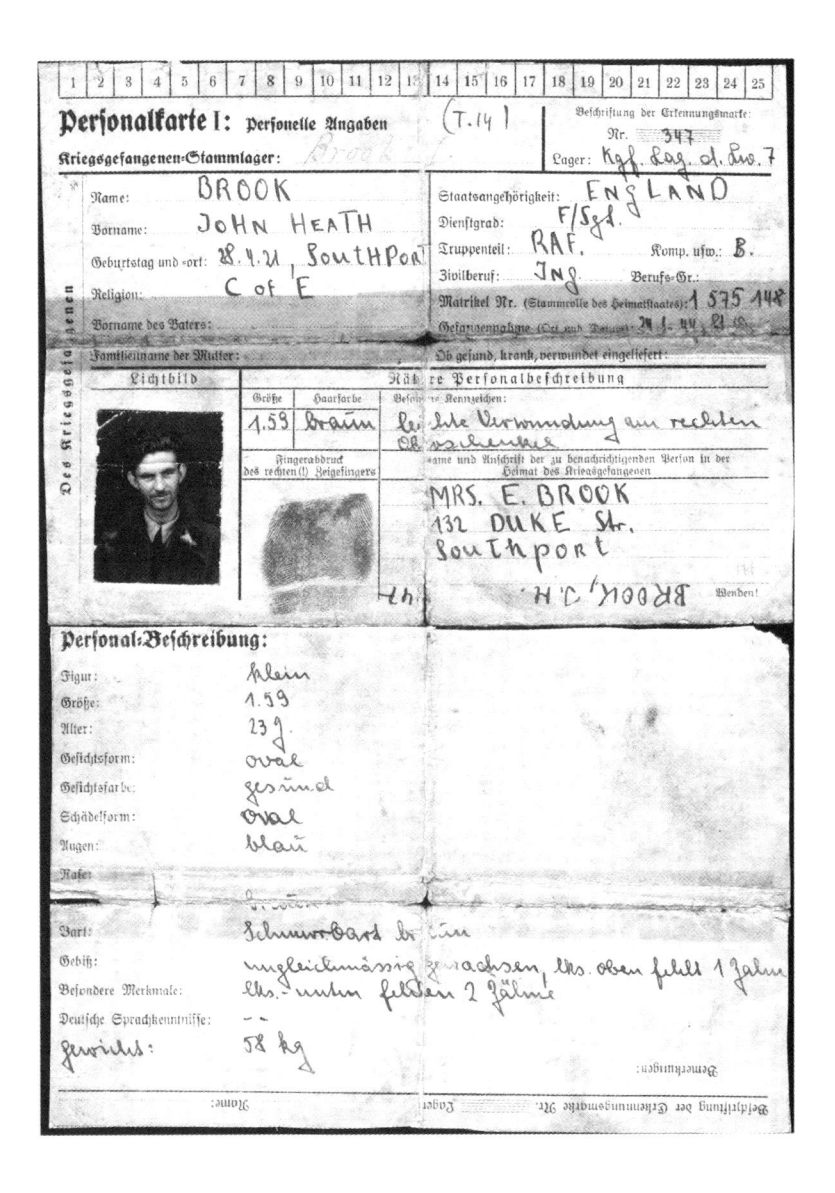

1	2	3	4	5	6	7	8	9	10	11	12	13	14	15	16	17	18	19	20	21	22	23	24	25

Personalkarte I: Personelle Angaben (T.14)

Beschriftung der Erkennungsmarke:
Nr. 347

Kriegsgefangenen-Stammlager: Brook

Lager: Kgf. Lag. d. Lw. 7

Name: BROOK
Vorname: JOHN HEATH
Geburtstag und -ort: 28.4.21, Southport
Religion: C of E
Vorname des Vaters:
Familienname der Mutter:

Staatsangehörigkeit: ENGLAND
Dienstgrad: F/Sgt.
Truppenteil: RAF. Komp. usw.: B.
Zivilberuf: Ing. Berufs-Gr.:
Matrikel Nr. (Stammrolle des Heimatstaates): 1 575 148
Gefangennahme (Ort und Datum): M 1.44. 8.10.
Ob gesund, krank, verwundet eingeliefert:

Lichtbild
Größe: 1.59
Haarfarbe: braun
Besondere Kennzeichen: leichte Verwundung am rechten Oberschenkel

Fingerabdruck des rechten (l.) Zeigefingers

Name und Anschrift der zu benachrichtigenden Person in der Heimat des Kriegsgefangenen:
MRS. E. BROOK
132 DUKE St.
Southport

BROOK, J.H. Wenden!

Personal-Beschreibung:
Figur: klein
Größe: 1.59
Alter: 23 J.
Gesichtsform: oval
Gesichtsfarbe: gesund
Schädelform: oval
Augen: blau
Nase:
Bart: Schnurrbart braun
Gebiß: ungleichmäßig gewachsen, lks. oben fehlt 1 Zahn, lks. unten fehlen 2 Zähne
Besondere Merkmale:
Deutsche Sprachkenntnisse: --
Gewicht: 58 kg

Bemerkungen:

Name; Lager; Beglaubigung der Erkennungsmarke Nr.

| **Dulag-Luft.** Kriegsgefangenenkartei. | Gefangenen-Erkennungsmarke Nr. 397 | Dulag-Luft Eingeliefert am: 14.7.44 |

NAME: B R O O K
Vornamen: John Heath
Dienstgrad: F/Sgt. **Funktion:** Bomb.
Matrikel-No.: 1.575.148
Geburtstag: 28.8.21
Geburtsort: Southport
Religion: C of E.
Zivilberuf: Ing.
Staatsangehörigkeit: britisch

Vorname des Vaters:
Familienname der Mutter:
Verheiratet mit:
Anzahl der Kinder:

Heimatanschrift:
Mrs. E. Brook
132 Duke Str.
Southport

Abschuß am 24.6.44 **bei:** St.Omers **Flugzeugtyp:** Lanc.
Gefangennahme am: w.o. **bei:** w.o.

Nähere Personalbeschreibung

Figur: klein
Größe: 162 cm
Schädelform: oval
Haare: braun
Gewicht: 58 kg
Gesichtsform: oval
Gesichtsfarbe: gesund

Augen: blau
Nase: normal
Bart: Schnurrbart braun
Gebiß: ungleichmässig gewachsen

Besondere Kennzeichen:
1. Verwundung am r. Oberschenkel

Front | Profil | Fingerabdruck

pressed, the Camp Leaders merely repeated that as far as they knew, negotiations were in progress, and they reminded us of the Commander in Chief's instructions for all PoWs to remain where they were until they received official instructions. The lack of action began to weigh heavily on us and we became very impatient. Our original estimate of two weeks was going to be well wide of the mark, and it seemed to us that our own people were just not making enough effort to get us out and back home. We tried to put it to the back of our minds and carried on as normally as possible, but it was not easy and the sole topic of conversation hinged on when we would be going home. The whole thing was beginning to smell of red tape and officialdom. Luckily, the foraging parties were continuing to do a good job and the improved soup ration was being maintained, otherwise morale would have dropped considerably.

The days continued to pass by with the Camp Leaders under ever increasing flak from prisoners, but in all fairness to them they knew no more than us and were just as anxious to get home. The Allied High Command must have been well aware that there were thousands of prisoners in a very poor physical and mental condition who were in need of advanced medical care. We began to suspect that we were the pawns in some political game between the Allies and the Russians.

Our fears were apparently justified a few days later when completely out of the blue, it was announced that the Russians could no longer allow us to accompany them on the food excursions, and they regretted that the soup ration would have to be reduced due to chronic food shortages. Worse was to follow. The following day it was announced that the guard towers would be manned once more, and the main gates locked at all times. It seemed as if we were back to square one.

The besieged Camp Leaders took the brunt of our feelings over this latest set back. It was hard for us to accept that one moment the Russians were friendly, and then could suddenly do an about turn. The Leaders made representations to the Russians but

Freedom (or is it?)

got nowhere, except to be told it was for our own safety as there was still fighting going on in the area. We did not believe this lame excuse for one moment. One thing was certain however, it emphasised the unstable situation that existed at the time between the east and the west and how unpredictable the Russians could be. I think it proved conclusively that we had been right to mistrust them.

One rumour that had been gathering momentum over the last few days was that the Americans had established a bridgehead over the River Elbe, some fifty kilometres away but had been prevented from advancing any further. This strengthened our fears that we were pig-in-the-middle of some political manoeuvring. We seemed to be in a no-man's land between the Russians and the Western allies and no one seemed to want to take responsibility for us. In the meantime our physical and mental condition was getting worse.

About two weeks after the arrival of the Russians, we heard that units of the American forces had managed to make contact with beleaguered Luckenwalde. The rumour was so persistent that Bill and I began to believe that there might be some truth in it after all, but when we later heard that the Americans were going to send trucks to within a few miles of the camp in order to start evacuating us, we once again became sceptical.

We decided to make enquiries from the American compound and walked around the perimeter to see if there were any visible signs of departure. Sure enough, we noticed what appeared to be a loose coil of wire in the perimeter fence in one corner. We sat down some distance away to await developments. After a while, two Americans approached, stepped over the trip wire, pulled the loose coil to one side and scrambled through, pulling it back after them. They then quickly walked across a field, keeping close to a hedgerow before turning left along a minor road and disappearing out of view. Shortly afterwards two others arrived and repeated the operation. We watched the guard towers but the guards could either not see them, or more likely, didn't want to. Altogether we watched about thirty men escape.

One thing that bothered me was that nobody could be certain that the escaping PoWs had contacted the Americans or not. They might have fallen foul of Russian or German troops still fighting in the area. It was a confusing situation and one that needed careful thought. Why would the Americans lay on this cloak and dagger affair, if indeed it was true? We decided to wait three more days just in case something official was announced.

We discussed what we would do if the American trucks turned out to be a myth. We decided there could be no coming back, and that we should walk on towards the River Elbe and try and make contact with the Americans that way. If they were still on the far side of the river, then we were in deep trouble. It was about fifty kilometres to the nearest point on the Elbe and we knew we were not in the best of shape to undertake such a walk, but we would have to risk it.

Bill decided to sell some of his sketches to the affluent prisoners for chocolate and dried fruit which we hoped would keep us going. We could always supplement our diet with vegetables from the fields as we had done on the march from Bankau. Fortunately, the weather was getting better. I kept tabs on the escape route to see if anybody returned, but nobody did.

The three days elapsed and we made our preparations. We had not made the decision to leave lightly. Apart from disobeying orders to stay put, we were also going against the principle of 'sticking together'. We gave the hammer to the man in the next bed with whom we had confided about our plans, but we decided to take the knife in case we had to pick vegetables.

After a sleepless night, we ate all the day's bread ration as soon as the orderlies brought it. We then draped our blankets round

Freedom (or is it?)

our shoulders, donned capes and hoods, picked up our rucksacks and left the billet.

At a barrack block just past the escape point, we stopped and pretended to enter into a conversation with each other. After about ten minutes two figures arrived, looked around furtively, and went through the wire. We waited five minutes to give them a head start, glanced either way, stepped over the trip wire, and made for the coil of wire. My heart was pumping wildly, and although it was a chilly morning, I felt hot and clammy. I went first, followed by Bill, who pulled the wire back into place. We walked across the field, keeping close to the hedgerow. It seemed to take an eternity to reach the tarmac road, but in reality it could only have been about one minute. I was expecting a fusillade of shots from the guard towers but nothing happened, and resisting the temptation to run, we turned left in single file along the road in a westerly direction. The die was cast and there was no way back now.

20

RENDEZVOUS

We silently followed in the footsteps of our colleagues up ahead, but not wishing to catch up with them. Glancing back, I saw three more figures following us. We must have walked for over two hours, and were beginning to think that the trucks were a myth after all, when we turned a bend and saw a stationary truck in the distance. We saw the two prisoners in front waving their arms in salute, and then breaking into a run. We were tempted to do the same, but could not be sure if the truck was American or not so decided to proceed with caution.

However, as we got nearer we saw the two prisoners ahead of us climbing over the tail board. Immediately I felt a huge weight lifting from my shoulders, and we had to restrain ourselves from cheering and shouting with joy. A coloured American with an automatic weapon was standing in the road and he told us to get into the truck and keep down low. We waited until the three men behind us arrived before driving off to freedom.

It is hard to describe my feelings at that moment, but the initial one was of relief, followed by gratitude to those American lads who were taking the trouble to get us out. As we drove on another lorry passed us, presumably to take our place at the rendezvous point. The soldier confirmed that they had been running this shuttle service for two weeks and had moved over three hundred Allied prisoners to safety. I told him word was getting around, and he could expect more customers from now on. He grinned and said that was the object of the exercise. He knew that the camp was in a state of siege, but did not know where the order had come from to send trucks to evacuate us. They had been told to go no nearer than six miles from the camp to avoid any incidents with the Russians. It seemed like an unofficial operation to me.

Eventually we crossed a Bailey bridge over the river and our truck rumbled slowly over it, making a loud metallic noise. Nearby, a smaller permanent bridge appeared to have been destroyed by fighting. We stopped at an airfield with several Dakota aircraft at the dispersal points. I wondered if we were going to be flown direct to Britain from here.

In actual fact, we were to be flown to a reception centre for repatriated prisoners of war near to Brussels. There we would receive new underwear and shirts and get a good night's sleep. He said he realised that we were limited in what we could eat, but hoped that coffee and cookies would be OK!

More and more prisoners were arriving and I was more than ever convinced that the Russians must have been under orders to shut their eyes to what was going on. I found it hard to believe that close on three hundred men could walk out of a camp in broad daylight without somebody knowing about it. Equally I was firmly of the opinion that the Allied leaders in the camp were fully aware of what the score was. My thoughts turned to the comrades we had left behind, to their frustrations and anger, and at the indifference displayed by our own people in High Command.

There were now enough of us to fill the transport plane. It seemed strange to be boarding a plane as passengers, and I settled back to enjoy the flight. At the reception centre we were deloused, allowed to shower and shave, and received the promised new items of clothing. We British would stay overnight before being flown to Cosford Aerodrome in England, where we would be debriefed, medically examined and then sent home on indefinite leave. The cheers rang out around the hangar! We enjoyed a light meal, and then climbed between the clean sheets, thinking this was luxury indeed.

On the flight to Cosford the following day, the pilot invited us one by one to come up to the front and catch our last glimpse of Europe's coast line. I remember thinking that the North Sea looked just as inhospitable as ever, and for a moment the old feeling of concern which I had experienced every time I flew over the North Sea during my operational days returned.

But when I caught my first glimpse of the white cliffs of Dover, I had a lump in my throat. There had been times when I had doubted that I would ever see England again, especially during those dark days of the forced march, but I had survived, and would soon be back on English soil.

21

JOURNEY'S END

Upon landing, my earliest recollection is seeing teams of smiling ladies from the WVS, YWCA and the Salvation Army manning trolleys with tea and sandwiches. At the debriefing session, an RAF Intelligence Officer asked which camps I had been held in, and what sort of treatment I had received at their hands. He passed no comment when I related my experiences at the interrogation centre, but appeared particularly interested in the period covering the march and the cattle trucks. He asked if any one had died during the march. I had to tell him that I didn't hear of any cases, but that so many men were at death's door that there may have been deaths later.

Strangely, he never asked how I came to be repatriated by the Americans when Luckenwalde had been relieved by the Russians. I was thankful that I was spared any embarrassing explanations as to how I 'escaped', but he seemed to have taken it for granted that the camp had been handed over to the Americans. I was tempted to ask for the official explanation as to why there had been such a delay in repatriating the prisoners, but on reflection decided to keep quiet. I never did find out.

Many years later, in the early 1990s, I read a newspaper article which referred to the possibility that after the war some 30,000 prisoners may have disappeared from German PoW camps after being put on boats for Russia. A German eye-witness claim to have seen 900 Allied troops in a Siberian prison camp in 1947.

At the medical, I was deeply aware of my gaunt appearance, but the nurse sensed my embarrassment and told me not to worry as all PoWs were facing the same problem. I had lost over two and a half stone, and it was highly likely that just after the march I must have weighed less than six stone.

The doctor stressed that I would need extra food and a special milk diet to enable me to start putting on some of my lost weight, but that I must be prepared for it to take a long time. I would be entitled to extra milk, eggs and other foods that were still on ration. I was given a leaflet on the dangers of overloading the stomach, but thought best not to tell him about the bread pudding episode. I was to put myself under the care of my local doctor when I got home, but my progress would be monitored by RAF doctors from time to time. He warned that I might suffer from bouts of depression, but this was a normal reaction.

I was also entitled to new uniform before returning home. This experience was a total contrast to when we first received our uniform. There was no one shouting and bawling at us this time, and we were treated like VIPs. I was only too glad to dispose of my filthy and ragged uniform, but before doing so remembered to retrieve my toy dog mascot which had accompanied me through all my operations and life as a PoW. I placed it reverently in my pocket. I also rescued my diary, which despite getting wet several times, was still readable. I was genuinely sorry to say goodbye to the flying boots which had served me so well, and my cape and hood.

On receiving my pay book, I found I had been promoted to Warrant Officer during my confinement in Germany. The promotion had been in the pipe line prior to my being shot down, and everything had been backdated. Things were moving at such a rapid pace that I was becoming a little overwhelmed. Life in a PoW camp runs at a leisurely pace and it was going to be a long time before I became accustomed to the hurly burly of everyday life again.

Journey's End

I met up with Bill once more and we collected six weeks pay as an interim payment. I then took my place in the queue for the telephone. Ironically, RAF Cosford was close to Wolverhampton and I wondered if any of my former colleagues from the telephone engineering department at Wolverhampton had been involved in their installation!

The phone seemed to ring out for ages. I recognised my mother's voice and I mumbled "Hello, Mum, it's me!" or something similar. It was an emotional moment and I could tell my mother was in tears. We did not say a lot to one another. There was no need to, even if we could have managed it.

The following morning it was the parting of the ways for Bill and me. Bill was going south to London, whilst I would be catching the Liverpool train. We shook hands and wished each other well. I waved to him until his train disappeared from view. We promised to keep in touch, but as so often happens, the years rolled by and we lost contact.

As I settled into the corner of the train carriage I tried to make myself as inconspicuous as possible. I had the uneasy feeling that people were looking at my gaunt appearance. I was the only serviceman in the carriage and thought that I stuck out like a sore thumb. I realise now that I was just being overly self conscious, but the feeling lasted for many weeks.

I had to change trains to get home to Southport, and my weakened arms soon ached from carrying my kit bag as I walked across Liverpool city centre to Exchange Street station. I was shattered.

On the journey to Southport I could see the destruction of Liverpool all around me. On either side of the track were empty shells which had once been warehouses and homes. Germany had not been alone in suffering aerial attacks, and all the visible destruction only served to emphasise the futility of war.

In no time at all it seemed the taxi driver was dropping me off at our house, and he helped me out of the taxi with my kit bag. He asked me if I was a repatriated prisoner of war, which did my morale no good at all, but I realised he was only trying to be friendly. I asked him the fare, but he waved his arms and said, "Have this one on me, lad!" before speeding off down the road.

I opened the gate and my eyes turned to the front door. The brass knocker in the guise of a Welsh lady was still there, well polished and sparkling. My heart was thumping wildly, as I walked down the path. I was home at long last and for me at least, the war was over.

Epilogue

In May 1987 I was privileged, along with my wife José, to attend the dedication service of the War Memorial at Woodhall Spa, Lincolnshire - the final war time home of 617 Squadron. It is constructed in the form of a dam and is an imposing monument, built in remembrance of all the members of the Squadron who lost their lives in World War II.

It was an emotional experience to read the names of all the men inscribed on the memorial, especially those of my former comrades and crew mates.

I was overjoyed however to meet up once more with Gerry Hobbs and his wife Nan. This was the first time we had met since being shot down. The last time I had seen Gerry was on a stretcher in Lille on his way to hospital. I was also elated to meet again the two remaining original members of the crew, Bobby McCullough and Ronnie Pooley, who was there with his wife Mavis and daughter Natalie.

Ronnie Pooley was our replacement for Red Cassaubon, our original Mid Upper Gunner, who was involved in that horrendous crash on takeoff. He made a full recovery only to go missing many months later with his new crew. Lorne Pritchard, who I also had not seen since being on that truck in Lille, survived the war and returned to Canada, but passed away some years later

During the day we were introduced to Sammy Isherwood's younger sister, Gwen Russell and her family. We had exchanged correspondence and spoken over the phone, but it was nice to meet face to face.

We all had a wonderful if somewhat emotional day, which even the almost constant torrential rain could not dampen.

L/R: Jack Brook, Ron Pooley, Gerry Hobbs, Bobby McCullough

In 1996 we were all saddened to hear from Bobby McCullough's wife, Betty, that he had passed away after a long illness, bravely endured. He will be sadly missed, along with Teddy the Skipper, Pritch, Red, Sammy, Bill, Ian and Tom.

In September 1996 I was at last able to fulfill a long standing desire to visit the graves of my comrades in France. Accompanied by my wife José and a friend who kindly volunteered to drive us, we first

Epilogue

visited the graves of Teddy, Sammy and Tom at Leulinghem. We later made our way to the War Graves Cemetery at Longuenesse where Ian and Bill are buried. The graves are beautifully kept by the staff of the War Graves Commission and it gives me great comfort to know that they are lovingly cared for and in safe hands.

Leulinghem ~ September 1996